SHADOW

TOUCHING THE DARKNESS WITHIN

Introduction by Robert Bly

JEREMY P. TARCHER/PUTNAM
A MEMBER OF PENGUIN PUTNAM INC.
NEW YORK

A Book Laboratory Book

Most Tarcher/Putnam books are available at special quantity discounts for bulk purchase for sales promotions, premiums, fund-raising, and educational needs. Special books or book excerpts also can be created to fit specific needs. For details, write Putnam Special Markets, 375 Hudson Street, New York, NY 10014.

Jeremy P. Tarcher/Putnam
A member of
Penguin Putnam Inc.
375 Hudson Street
New York, NY 10014
www.penguinputnam.com
Introduction © Robert Bly
Touching Our Darkness Through Stories and Art © Mark Robert Waldman
Designed by Kristen Garneau, Garneau Design, Sausalito, CA

Library of Congress Cataloging-in-Publications Data

Shadow: searching for the hidden self / introduction by Robert Bly.
          p. cm.—(Archetypes of the collective unconscious ; v. 1)
       "A Book Laboratory book"—T.p. verso
     ISBN 1-58542-191-X
        1. American literature. 2. Archetype (Psychology)—Literary collections. 3.
     Self-realization—Literary collections. 4. Subconsciousness—Literary
     collections. I. Series.
   PS509.A73S53 2002   2002028703
 810.8'0353—dc21

Printed in Singapore
10 9 8 7 6 5 4 3 2 1

TABLE OF CONTENTS

OUR WORLD IS FILLED WITH ARCHETYPAL IMAGERY, POWERFUL SYMBOLS THAT REFLECT THE DEEPEST LAYERS OF OUR personality—our strengths, weaknesses, and unacknowledged gifts that lay hidden within our souls. Primarily unconscious, these inner forces shape our behaviors, attitudes and beliefs. By exploring these secret desires—in ourselves, through literature and art—we can gain mastery over them, bringing greater consciousness into our lives.

Archetypal themes are universal, for they can be found in every culture throughout history. But each society reflects them in distinctive ways. The American lover, for example, is far more romantic, erotic, and idealized than the images portrayed in Asia. By contrast, the shadow, which is aptly acknowledged in the European psyche, is relatively ignored by Americans. Unlike other cultures, we do not like to peer directly at the darkness that lies within. Instead we project our shadows onto fiction, the movies, or the criminal elements in the world. Even the shadow artists in America are often met with hostility or disdain, especially when the subject offends our moral and religious values. The shadow artist is readily condemned, an unpatriotic pariah that spoils our fantasies and dreams.

The American seeker is also unique amongst the cultures of the world: in our separation of church from state, religion becomes a quest for personal spirituality, one that liberally borrows from other traditions and groups. Our economic and scientific advancements have also transformed the healer archetype from a country shaman into a medical sage.

Artists, poets, and writers help to bring these archetypal forms to life by embracing them in their work. Stephen King, for example, is a master of the shadow, as was Sexton, Poe, and Melville. The spiritual quest of the seeker is vividly captured in the poetry of Whitman and Frost, in the prose of Alice Walker, and in the speeches of Martin Luther King. Even the face of Andrew Weil, alternative medicine's champion, has become a core archetypal symbol of the American healer: wise, warm, and passionately devoted to the integration of body, mind, and soul. And who would not be moved by O. Henry's *The Gift of the Magi* in which two lovers sacrifice their most valued possessions to soothe each other's heart.

Art in particular makes a strong impression upon our soul, and in choosing the illustrations to accompany these stories, we have selected unique images that span the breadth and depth of contemporary American painting and photography. From the sun-dappled colors of the impressionists, to the austere contrasts of black and white photography, and from the immediacy of the advertising medium and the obliqueness of the symbolic form, these images hint at the acuity of our inner landscapes and dreams. Mysterious, moody, and serene, they work upon our psyches inviting us to rest the eye upon the symbolic eloquence of life.

May these stories and images guide you inwards as you witness that wondrous place where a greater consciousness resides.

The wonder of the collective unconscious is that it is all there, all the legend and history of the human race, with its unexorcised demons and its gentle saints, its mysteries and its wisdom, all with each one of us—a microcosm with the macrocosm. The exploration of this world is more challenging than the exploration of the solar system; and the journey to inner space is not necessarily an easy or a safe trip.

—June Singer

The archetype represents a profound riddle surpassing our rational comprehension [expressing] itself first and foremost in metaphors. There is some part of its meaning that always remains unknown and defies formulation.

—Jacobi Jolande

Our personal psychology is just a thin skin, a ripple on the ocean of collective psychology [and] the archetypes are the great decisive forces, they bring about the real events, and not our personal reasoning and practical intellect. . . . The archetypal images decide the fate of man.

—Carl G. Jung

Series Editor: Mark Robert Waldman
Series conceived by Jeremy P. Tarcher
Series created by Philip Dunn, Manuela Dunn Mascetti and Book Laboratory
Picture research by Julie Foakes
Design by Kristen Garneau

Other Titles in the Series:
Healer: Transforming Our Inner and Outer Wounds, Volume 2, with an Introduction by Andrew Weil
Seeker: Traveling the Path to Enlightenment, Volume 3, with an Introduction by Jean Houston
Lover: Embracing Our Passionate Hearts, Volume 4, with an Introduction by Robert A. Johnson

T H R E E   V I E W S   O F   T H E   S H A D O W

Introduction by Robert Bly

THE SHADOW IS NOT A PLEASANT SUBJECT TO TALK ABOUT. HUMAN BEINGS HAVE NEVER WANTED TO TALK MUCH about their dark side. If they had wanted to, it wouldn't now be called the shadow. There's a habit of thought and feeling called ascensionism, in which we worship the light-filled Gods and Goddesses, assuring each other that human beings are really good people—a little distorted by bad political arrangements, perhaps—but inhabitors of a world in which grief and sorrow are mistaken emotions, and the earth is a beneficent deity. In ascensionist mythology, volcanoes are aberrations and the destructive Shiva does not exist, nor Kali and Baba Yaga.

We ordinarily try to pass quickly over the dark events that have happened to us. All dark episodes "happened" to us. We weren't part of it. I don't know why I go on criticizing such a human being because I've been a person like that much of my life. For many years I've written upward-looking poetry. It's possible that men and women in their thirties or even early forties don't have the psychic equipment to look at their own shadow.

The word shadow clearly implies that when the sun falls on us, particularly in early morning or late evening, anyone watching will see a long shadow shaped exactly like us. Since we rarely look behind us, the word shadow implies a part of us that is hidden to others, and perhaps to ourselves. Robert Louis Stevenson tried to bring this complicated hiddenness into Dr. Jekyll and Mr. Hyde.

When William Booth and I put together a few years ago, *A Little Book on the Human Shadow*, we imagined the shadow as a sort of bag into which we insert early on parts of ourselves that our parents or teachers don't like. At four or five we might put our noisiness into this bag; and later put in our infantile and juvenile angers, our sexual curiosities, our recklessness, our high spirits and our ability to dance. We spend the first twenty years of our life putting things into the bag, and the rest of our life trying to get them back out again. This bag we might call the personal shadow.

The word shadow also points to a bundle of impulses thousands and thousands of years old that, when evoked, will be happy to beat children, murder neighbors, burn holy books and Celtic priests, exterminate the Cheyenne, carpet-bomb ancient cities, torture old friends, sacrifice sons, daughters, lambs, goats, or a thousand young men all in one day to keep our religion pure, or to bring about better weather. I mentioned the long age of the shadow so that we won't imagine that by throwing light on our shadow in a book like this we can bring about much change in the short term. The shadow is ineradicable. It is 400,000 years old. It can easily skirt around all sorts of moral directives and Buddhist insights.

This bundle of ominous impulses, thousands of years old, clearly inherited from our animal or "primitive" past, was given to us by our ancestors. It flows in from their dark side. We know that we receive light-filled and spiritual gifts from our cultural ancestors as well. We could call this bundle of ominous impulses the historical or community shadow.

In the last ten years, brain researchers have contributed a third view of the shadow, by suggesting a possibility once considered utterly out of the question, namely, the idea that human beings possess a two-brain system. The primary brain, so to speak, accomplishes all the practical labors, chopping wood, making tools, cooking food, typing reports; but the researchers suspect there is also a separate organ in the brain that stores trauma. Some believe that the small horseshoe-shaped organ in the brain called the *amygdala* is the storage place. The trauma is stored there in such a way that is inaccessible to the primary brain, and so to consciousness. This dodge may have been a survival necessity. Our ancestors might have experienced a massacre of their small group, or by many people in it, by a hostile tribe or by animals or by some natural disaster, and "forgetting" the trauma would have helped to keep the survivors from dying of grief or shock. The phrase "altered states" is associated with those moments when the trauma leaks through. Therapy, because it uses the language of the primary brain, may not reach the amygdala. This idea helps explain why the healing of severely abused children turns out to be more difficult than people once believed. It also helps explain the difficulty of keeping early childhood traumas from destroying marriage relationships thirty years later. Moreover, the concept helps to explain multiple personalities, in which separate personalities can secretly co-exist and operate independently from the main personality, the one we would usually identify as "me" or "I". Finally, it throws light on the turmoil of Vietnam veterans, who are experiencing "flashbacks" or what Martin Prachtel calls "unmetabolized grief."

If, over the last 400,000 years every act of violence our ancestors witnessed or participated in is stored in some remote place away from the forward-looking, ascencionist, or speaking brain, it's no wonder that many of us want to live our lives without looking at our shadow at all.

I've sketched here, in an inadequate way, three separate views of the human shadow. The investigation of the human shadow, which is a strong and admirable part of our twentieth century labors, may be the most important work we can do at this historical moment, when the computer seems to offer us a past made of clean, even antiseptic, information. Global capitalism's proponents try to overlook the extermination of cultures that capitalism's shadow delights in.

America is in a dangerous spot now in relation to the shadow. Capitalism has defeated socialism, and is now on it's way to defeat culture. In the last twenty years, serious reviewers have disappeared in the United States, along with study in High School. The American system encourages mass childishness. The American people have elected a childish president, George W Bush, who is unable to stand against the oil and timber industries, the Lords of shadow.

All literature, both of the primitive and the modern peoples, can be thought of as creations by the "dark side" to enable it to rise up from the earth and join in the sunlight of consciousness again. Such American writers as Hawthorne, Poe, Melville, Eliot and Frost did much shadow work, both in their personal lives and in their writing; and we still have to turn today to poets and writers for the truth about the shadow. W.B. Yeats, sensing global capitalism, said:

> *What rough beast, it's hour come round at last,*
> *Slouches toward Bethlehem to be born?*

And Cesar Vallejo says:

> *Well, on the day I was born,*
> *God was sick..*

The American poet William Stafford said in *A Ritual to Read to Each Other:*

*If you don't know the kind of person I am
and I don't know the kind of person you are
a pattern that others made may prevail in the world
and following the wrong god home we may miss our star.*

*For there is many a small betrayal in the mind,
a shrug that let's the fragile sequence break
sending with shouts the horrible errors of childhood
storming out to play through the broken dyke.*

*And as elephants parade holding each elephant's tail,
but if one wanders the circus won't find the park,
I call it cruel and maybe the root of all cruelty
to know what occurs but not to recognize the fact.*

*And so I appeal to a voice, to something shadowy,
a remote important region in all who talk:
though we could fool each other, we should consider—
lest the parade of our mutual life get lost in the dark.*

*For it is important that awake people be awake,
or a breaking line may discourage them back to sleep;
the signals we give—yes or no, or maybe—
should be clear: the darkness around us is deep.*

Above: Chester Arnold, *Genealogy*

Projection [helps] explain the immense popularity of horror novels and movies. Through a vicarious enactment of the shadow side, our evil impulses can be stimulated and perhaps relieved in the safety of the book or theater.

—Connie Zweig and
Jeremiah Abrams

T O U C H I N G   O U R   D A R K N E S S   T H R O U G H   S T O R I E S   A N D   A R T

by Mark Robert Waldman, Series Editor

Throughout history the shadow has appeared via the human imagination as a monster, a dragon, a Frankenstein, a white whale, an extraterrestrial, or a man so vile that we cannot see ourselves in him; he is as removed from us as a gorgon. Revealing the dark side of human nature has been, then, one of the primary purposes of art and literature. As Nietzsche puts it: "We have art so that we shall not die of reality.

—Connie Zweig and Jeremiah Abrams, *Meeting the Shadow*

From Edgar Allan Poe to Stephen King, in our fiction, poetry and art, images of the shadow have permeated our fantasies and fears. But though our literature is rich with archetypal symbolism, we, as individuals, often shy away from taking a closer look within, hesitating to embrace the shadows that we find. Outwardly, we are fascinated with the shadow, but inwardly, we often deny its existence.

The shadow is a moral problem that challenges everyone, wrote Carl Jung, for it requires considerable effort to bring it into awareness. It is painful to admit that we have shortcomings—that our personalities are flawed, that we feel moments of genuine hate, anxiety, weakness and greed—and when they erupt, we quickly sweep them away and ignore their power for abuse. Only through careful self-reflection and a modicum of courage can we discern the darker realms of the soul. The benefits are great, for it gives us power to redirect our destructiveness into acts of goodness and strength, knowledge and strength. But if we ignore our shadow side, it may slip out unexpectedly, bringing chaos and personal grief, a theme that is brought to life in Hans Christian Andersen's tale. Listen:

It begins with a man—a philosopher and poet—who is suddenly startled from sleep. Peering out through his window, he sees his shadow slink across the street and disappear into a brothel. The next morning his shadow returns and begs for freedom. The scholar sees no reason to refuse, and so the shadow takes his leave.

Years passed and the learned man grew weak. He seemed on the edge of death when his shadow returned to visit. No longer dark and formless, he had taken on the trappings of aristocracy, complete with flowing robes and a gold pouch by his side.

"My dear man," the shadow said. "You look so pale and ill."

"That is so," the learned man replied. "But you appear to have done very well."

"Life has treated me favorably, I must admit. Why don't you join me in my travels? The journey will refresh your soul."

"I am honored," said the man, and so their adventure began. But the shadow was master now, and the master became the shadow.

One day, they came upon a beautiful princess, and the shadow asked for her hand. "But you have no shadow!" the princess exclaimed, looking suspiciously at the strange man.

Pointing to the man by his side, the shadowy figure replied, "I have given my shadow permission to stand on his own, and have provided him with fine clothes to wear.

"This foreigner's customs are strange," the princess thought, "but he is powerful and rich. Together we might rule the countryside."

"Come home with me," she said, "and we shall discuss a wedding plan."

When they reached the palace gates, the princess left her fiancee standing near the guards. The shadow turned and whispered to the man, "You can stay with me, and live in luxury, but on our wedding day you must lie at my feet as my shadow."

"This is absurd!" the learned man complained. "I shall tell the princess the truth."

But the shadow called for the guards and had the man imprisoned.

"You tremble," said the princess, when the shadow appeared by her side. "Has anything happened? You must not be ill today, on the eve of our wedding feast."

"Dear princess! I have just been through a terrible ordeal, for my shadow has gone mad. I suppose that having such a poor, shallow brain was too much for him to bear. He fancies that he has become a real man, and that I am his shadow."

"How terrible," the princess moaned. "Did you lock him up?"

"Oh yes, certainly, for I fear he will never recover."

"You were so kind," the princess said, "to give him freedom from his frail existence. But look what happens: You try to raise the lower class, and they flounder and slip in despair. You have done the right thing by putting him away."

"It is hard," said the shadow, heaving a pretentious sigh, "for he was a faithful servant."

"Yours is a noble character," said the princess, and she bowed deeply to her prince.

In the evening, cannons were fired and the soldiers presented their arms. It was indeed a grand wedding, but the learned man heard nothing of these affairs, for he had already been put to death.

Myths and fairy tales have often been used to describe the shadows we harbor inside. But today, many parents try to protect their children—and themselves—from anything dark or grim. On a personal level, we ignore our potential for abuse: those quiet insults that so often lead to divorce. On a societal level, we turn our eyes from the poverty and suffering that plague that our inner cities, hesitating to invest in education and social reform. We may be the most democratic country in the world, but do we really accept differences of another person's religious or political beliefs? Will we sincerely fight for human values and rights, or will we hide our arrogance behind the flags of national pride? These are the demons that haunt our personal and cultural lives.

These are the issues that are pondered in stories that fill this book. In Nathaniel Hawthorne's *Young Goodman Brown*, we find the shadow lurking among the citizens of a seemingly moral town in the prudish schoolteacher, the innocent wife, and the self-righteous minister of the community church—all sneak out to drink the devil's brew. We taste the unrelenting hate of a man obsessed with revenge in Melville's *Moby Dick,* and we witness the uncontrollable guilt that festers in *The Telltale Heart* by Poe. In Frederick Douglas's *Diary of an American Slave,* we are reminded of the bigotry that continues to infect our lives, a theme that is fatally echoed in

Shirley Jackson's classic tale, *The Lottery*. On a more humorous note, we can smile at the darkness that permeates our spiritual and sexual urge with Howard Fast's *The Hand of God* and Risa Mickenberg's *Direct Male.*

Sexual yearning and betrayal are also themes of Malamud's tale, *The Model*, a story of a lonely painter who seeks the memory of lost love in a woman who is hired to pose nude. A paradox is raised in this tale: does the shadow reside in the eyes of the painter, or in the accusatory mood of the model, a woman who suspects that she is being violated by the artist's gaze? William Golding's *Lord of the Flies* confronts the reader with even darker questions: does a heart of blackness beat quietly in every boy and girl?

Finally, if we look closely, we may also discover that the shadow has a silver lining, for in our depths we hold the seeds of our untapped potentialities and gifts. In darkness, says Nelson Mandela, our finest qualities shine:

> *Our deepest fear is not that we are inadequate. Our deepest fear is that we are powerful beyond measure. It is our light, not our darkness, that most frightens us. We ask ourselves, who am I to be brilliant, gorgeous, talented, fabulous? Actually, who are you not to be? It is not just in some of us; it is in everyone. And as we let our own light shine, we unconsciously give other people permission to do the same.*

Through self-reflection and understanding, we can use our shadows to illuminate our strength.

Who knows what evil lurks in the hearts of men? The Shadow knows!

—From the radio series "The Shadow," first broadcast in August, 1930

RUMPELSTILTSKIN
Anne Sexton

INSIDE MANY OF US
is a small old man
who wants to get out.
No bigger than a two-year-old
whom you'd call lamb chop
yet this one is old and malformed.
His head is okay
but the rest of him wasn't Sanforized.
He is a monster of despair.
He is all decay.
He speaks up as tiny as an earphone
with Truman's asexual voice:
I am your dwarf.
I am the enemy within.
I am the boss of your dreams.
No. I am not the law in your mind,
the grandfather of watchfulness.
I am the law of your members,
the kindred of blackness and impulse.
See. Your hand shakes.
It is not palsy or booze.
It is your Doppelgänger
trying to get out.
Beware . . . Beware . . .

Left: Leonard Baskin, *The Old Artist.*

THE   MONSTER   NEVER   DIES

Stephen King
Excerpt from *Cujo*

ONCE UPON A TIME NOT SO LONG AGO, A MONSTER CAME TO THE SMALL TOWN OF Castle Rock, Maine. He killed a waitress named Aima Frechette in 1970; a woman named Pauline Toothaker and a junior high school student named Cheryl Moody in 1971; a pretty girl named Carol Dunbarger in 1974; a teacher named Etta Ringgold in the fall of 1975; finally, a grade-schooler named Mary Kate Hendrasen in the early winter of that same year.

He was not werewolf, vampire, ghoul, or unnameable creature from the enchanted forest or from the snowy wastes; he was only a cop named Frank Dodd with mental and sexual problems. A good man named John Smith uncovered his name by a

Above: A devil figure from the Burning Man Festival 2001, photograph by Tony Pletts. The devil is the ultimate monster. This piece of modern art demonstrates he is still alive and well, and living in the modern American psyche.   **Right:** Jane Zich, *Chained Melody.*

kind of magic, but before he could be captured—perhaps it was just as well—Frank Dodd killed himself.

There was some shock, of course, but mostly there was rejoicing in that small town, rejoicing because the monster which had haunted so many dreams was dead, dead at last. A town's nightmares were buried in Frank Dodd's grave.

Yet even in this enlightened age, when so many parents are aware of the psychological damage they may do to their children, surely there was one parent somewhere in Castle Rock—or perhaps one grandmother—who quieted the kids by telling them that Frank Dodd would get them if they didn't watch out, if they weren't good. And surely a hush fell as children looked toward their dark windows and thought of Frank Dodd in his shiny black vinyl raincoat, Frank Dodd who had choked . . . and choked . . . and choked.

He's out there, I can hear the grandmother whispering as the wind whistles down the chimney pipe and snuffles around the old pot lid crammed in the stove hole. *He's out there, and if you're not good, it may be* his *face you see looking in your bedroom window after everyone in the house is asleep except you; it may be* his *smiling face you see peeking at you from the closet in the middle of the night, the STOP sign he hold up when he crossed the little children in one hand, the razor he used to kill himself in the other . . . so shhh, children . . . shhhh . . . shhhh . . . .*

But for most, the ending was the ending. There were nightmares to be sure, and children who lay wakeful to be sure, and the empty Dodd house (for his mother had a stroke shortly afterwards and died) quickly gained a reputation as a haunted house and was avoided; but these were passing phenomena—the perhaps unavoidable side effects of a chain of senseless murders.

But time passed. Five years of time.

The monster was gone, the monster was dead. Frank Dodd moldered inside his coffin.

Except that the monster never dies. Werewolf, vampire, ghoul, unnameable creature from the wastes. The monster never dies.

It came to Castle Rock again in the summer of 1980.

T ad Trenton, four years old, awoke one morning not long after midnight . . . needing to go to the bathroom. He got out of bed and walked half asleep toward the white light thrown in a wedge through the half-open door, already lowering his pajama pants. He urinated forever, flushed, and went back to bed. He pulled the covers up, and that was when he saw the creature in his closet.

Low to the ground it was, with huge shoulders bulking above its cocked head, its eyes amber-glowing pits—a thing that might have been half man, half wolf. And its eyes rolled to follow him as he sat up, his scrotum crawling, his hair standing on end, his breath a thin winter-whistle in his throat: mad eyes that laughed, eyes that promised horrible death and the music of screams that went unheard; something in the closet.

He heard its purring growl; he smelled its sweet carrion breath.

Tad Trenton clapped his hands to his eyes, hitched in breath, and screamed.

A muttered exclamation in another room—his father.

A scared cry of "What was that?" from the same room—his mother.

Their footfalls, running. As they came in, he peered through his fingers and saw it there in the closet, snarling, promising dreadfully that they might come, but they would surely go, and that when they did—

The light went on. Vic and Donna Trenton came to his bed, exchanging a look of concern over his chalky face and his staring eyes, and his mother said—no, snapped, "I told you three hot dogs was too many, Vic!"

And then his daddy was on the bed, Daddy's arm around his back, asking him what was wrong.

Tad dared to look into the mouth of his closet again.

The monster was gone. Instead of whatever hungry beast he had seen, there were two uneven piles of blankets, winter bedclothes which Donna had not yet gotten around to taking up to the cut-off third floor. These were stacked on the chair which Tad used to stand on when he needed something from the high closet shelf. Instead of the shaggy, triangular head, cocked sideways in a kind of predatory questioning gesture, he saw his teddybear on the taller of the two piles of blankets. Instead of pitted and baleful amber eyes, there were the friendly brown glass balls from which his Teddy observed the world.

"What's wrong, Tadder?" his daddy asked him again.

"There was a monster!" Tad cried. "In my closet!" And he burst into tears.

His mommy sat with him; they held him between them, soothed him as best they could. There followed the ritual of parents. They explained there were no monsters; that he had just had a bad dream. His mommy explained how shadows could sometimes look like the bad things they sometimes showed on TV or in the comic books, and Daddy told him everything was all right, fine, that nothing in their good house could hurt him. Tad nodded and agreed that it was so, although he knew it was not.

His father explained to him how, in the dark, the two uneven piles of blankets had looked like hunched shoulders, how the teddybear had looked like a cocked head, and how the bathroom light, reflecting from Teddy's glass eyes, had made them seem like the eyes of a real live animal.

"Now look," he said. "Watch me close, Tadder."

Tad watched.

His father took the two piles of blankets and put them far back in Tad's closet. Tad could hear the coathangers jingling softly, talking about Daddy in their coathanger language. That was funny, and he smiled a little. Mommy caught his smile and smiled back, relieved.

His daddy came out of the closet, took Teddy, and put him in Tad's arms.

"And last but not least," Daddy said with a flourish and a bow that made both Tad and Mommy giggle, "ze chair."

He closed the closet door firmly and then put the chair against the door. When he came back to Tad's bed he was still smiling, but his eyes were serious.

"Okay, Tad?"

"Yes," Tad said, and then forced himself to say it. "But it was there, Daddy. I saw it. Really."

"Your *mind* saw something, Tad, "Daddy said, and his big, warm hand stroked Tad's hair. "But you didn't see a monster in your closet, not a real one. There are no monsters, Tad. Only in stories, and in your mind."

He looked from his father to his mother and back again—their big, well-loved faces.

"Really?"

"Really," his mommy said. "Now I want you to get up and go pee, big guy."

"I did. That's what woke me up."

"Well," she said, because parents never believed you, "humor me then, what do you say?"

So he went in and she watched while he did four drops and she smiled and said, "See? You *did* have to go."

Resigned, Tad nodded. Went back to bed. Was tucked in. Accepted kisses.

And as his mother and father went back to the door the fear settled on him again like a cold coat full of mist. Like a shroud stinking of hopeless death. *Oh please*, he thought, but there was no more, just that: *Oh please oh please oh please.*

Right: Alfonso Ossorio, *Scavenger's Heart.*

Perhaps his father caught his thought, because Vic turned back, one hand on the light switch, and repeated: "No monsters, Tad."

"No, Daddy," Tad said, because in that instant his father's eyes seemed shadowed and far, as if he needed to be convinced. "No monsters." *Except for the one in my closet.*

The light snapped off.

"Good night, Tad." His mother's voice trailed back to him lightly, softly, and in his mind he cried out, *Be careful, Mommy, they eat the ladies! In all the movies they catch the ladies and carry them off and eat them! Oh please oh please oh please—*

But they were gone.

So Tad Trenton, four years old, lay in his bed, all wires and stiff Erector Set braces. He lay with the covers pulled up to his chin and one arm crushing Teddy against his chest, and there was Luke Skywalker on one wall; there was a chipmunk standing on a blender on another wall, grinning cheerily (IF LIFE HANDS YOU LEMONS, MAKE LEMONADE! the cheeky, grinning chipmunk was saying); there was the whole motley Sesame Street crew on a third: Big Bird, Bert, Ernie, Oscar, Grover. Good totems; good magic. But oh the wind outside, screaming over the roof and skating down black gutters! He would sleep no more this night.

But little by little the wires unsnarled themselves and stiff Erector Set muscles relaxed. His mind began to drift . . .

And then a new screaming, this one closer than the nightwind outside, brought him back to staring wakefulness again.

The hinges on the closet door.

Creeeeeeeeeeeeee—

That thin sound, so high that perhaps only dogs and small boys awake in the night could have heard it. His closet door swung open

Above: Jane Zich, *Into Dreams.*

slowly and steadily, a dead mouth opening on darkness inch by inch and foot by foot.

The monster was in that darkness. It crouched where it had crouched before. It grinned at him, and its huge shoulders bulked above its cocked head, and its eyes glowed amber, alive with stupid cunning. *I told you they'd go away*, Tad, it whispered. *They always do, in the end. And then I can come back. I like to come back. I like you, Tad. I'll come back every night now, I think, and every night I'll come a little closer to your bed . . . and a little closer . . . until one night, before you can scream for them, you'll hear something growling, something growling right beside you, Tad, it'll be me, and I'll pounce, and then I'll eat you and you'll be in me.*

Tad stared at the creature in his closet with drugged, horrified fascination. There was something that . . . was almost familiar.

Something he almost knew. And that was the worst, that almost knowing. Because—

Because I'm crazy, Tad. I'm here. I've been here all along. My name was Frank Dodd once, and I killed the ladies, and maybe I ate them, too. I've been here all along, I stick around, I keep my ear to the ground. I'm the monster, Tad, the old monster, and I'll have you soon, Tad. Feel me getting closer . . . and closer . . . .

Perhaps the thing in the closet spoke to him in its own hissing breath, or perhaps its voice was the wind's voice. Either way, neither way, it didn't matter. He listened to its words, drugged with terror, near fainting (but oh so wide awake); he looked upon its shadowed, snarling face, which he almost knew. He would sleep no more tonight; perhaps he would never sleep again.

But sometime later, sometime between the striking of half past midnight and the hour of one, perhaps because he was small, Tad drifted away again. Thin sleep in which hulking, furred creatures with white teeth chased him deepened into dreamless slumber.

The wind held long conversations with the gutters. A rind of white spring moon rose in the sky. Somewhere far away, in some still meadow of night or along some pine-edged corridor of forest, a dog barked furiously and then fell silent.

And in Tad Trenton's closet, something with amber eyes held watch.

A DARK FABLE

Joyce Carol Oates

THE CHILD VANISHED FROM her family's cottage by night. In the dawn, her little bed was empty. "Oh where is she? Our daughter, our baby? Who has taken her from us? "—so the distraught parents cried, for they knew that their daughter would not have left them of her own volition,

Left: Cathryn Chase, *Halloween Chill.*

but must have been abducted. Yet though they searched everywhere for her, and would never abandon their quest for the remainder of their unhappy lives, they would not find her. Had cruel fairies carried her off into the Underworld? Had a wild beast leapt through a window as everyone slept, and bore her away in his jaws? Or had the little girl simply vanished?—as dew sparkling like gems will vanish on the grass with the inexorable rising of the sun, transforming the night to day.

In fact the child had been abducted by fairies. But not carried into the Underworld. Her fate was more mysterious, and more cruel: she was bartered to a wealthy noble family who lived in a great house on a promontory above the village in which the little girl's family lived, their ancient name synonymous with high rank and devout Christian belief and the solemn responsibilities of such.

Oh, what had happened to her!—the little girl would never comprehend. She woke to find herself crudely bound and gagged; she was carried into the earth, to be freed in a dungeon beneath the great house; she would be given just enough food and drink to sustain her, and just enough candlelight for her to see dimly, as undersea creatures see with primitive eyes. At the outset of her confinement she wept and pleaded with her captors to be released, but her captors were servants of the noble family, and paid her no attention. She might have been pleading with the blank granite face of the mountain. She might have been pleading with the great Jehovah himself.

The noble family came to glimpse the child, through a grating in the dungeon door, only a few times. Enough for them to be assured by their servants that the little sacrifice was safely confined. "She is still alive. She eats, she drinks. She no longer walks, but she crawls. She has grown dull-witted. Her vision is poor. But she has ceased begging to be released. She has ceased crying. Like the others, she will forget, in time, the world beyond the dungeon that is now her home."

The noble family was content that the little sacrifice was a success.

"She is our measure of what God will allow. Without her, how could we gauge the wickedness in our hearts? And, in our hearts, in the heart of mankind? How could we gauge our own good fortune?"

The noble family looked upon their own innocent children with joy and gratitude.

These were good, generous Christian folk. Except for their single aberration, they were virtuous human beings. They attended Sunday church services without fail, they tithed from their considerable income, they gave to the poor, they were never without smiles and blessings for others less fortunate than themselves. Seeing each Sunday in church the grieving, broken parents of the little sacrifice, they were especially kind.

Left: Chester Arnold, *TWA Corbies*. Nature is defenseless in the face of man's technology and, faced with a choice between profit and destruction of nature, it is nature that is sacrificed. This painting shows environmental devastation.

T H E   L O T T E R Y

Shirley Jackson

THE MORNING OF JUNE 27TH WAS CLEAR AND SUNNY, WITH THE FRESH WARMTH OF A FULL-SUMMER DAY; THE flowers were blossoming profusely and the grass was richly green. The people of the village began to gather in the square, between the post office and the bank, around ten o'clock; in some towns there were so many people that the lottery took two days and had to be started on June 26th, but in this village, where there were only about three hundred people, the whole lottery took less than two hours, so it could begin at ten o'clock in the morning and still be through in time to allow the villagers to get home for noon dinner.

The children assembled first, of course. School was recently over for the summer, and the feeling of liberty sat uneasily on most of them; they tended to gather together quietly for a while before they broke into boisterous play, and their talk was still of the classroom and the teacher, of books and reprimands. Bobby Martin had already stuffed his pockets full of stones, and the other boys soon followed his example, selecting the smoothest and roundest stones; Bobby and Harry Jones and Dickie Delacroix—the villagers pronounced this name "Dellacroy"—eventually made a great pile of stones in one corner of the square and guarded it against the raids of the other boys. The girls stood aside, talking among themselves, looking over their shoulders at the boys, and the very small children rolled in the dust or clung to the hands of their older brothers or sisters.

Right: Chester Arnold, *After the Fall*. Chester Arnold is noted for art that elevates the catastrophic to an exalted level of profound beauty. In this painting, the people are in a fervor to get to their destination—through the dramatically beautiful landscape surrounding them—oblivious to the coming catastrophe.

Soon the men began to gather, surveying their own children, speaking of planting and rain, tractors and taxes. They stood together, away from the pile of stones in the corner, and their jokes were quiet and they smiled rather than laughed. The women, wearing faded house dresses and sweaters, came shortly after their menfolk. They greeted one another and exchanged bits of gossip as they went to join their husbands. Soon the women, standing by their husbands, began to call to their children, and the children came reluctantly, having to be called four or five times. Bobby Martin ducked under his mother's grasping hand and ran, laughing, back to the pile of stones. His father spoke up sharply, and Bobby came quickly and took his place between his father and his oldest brother.

The lottery was conducted—as were the square dances, the teenage club, the Halloween program—by Mr. Summers, who had time and energy to devote to civic activities. He was a round-faced, jovial man and he ran the coal business, and people were sorry for him, because he had no children and his wife was a scold. When he arrived in the square, carrying the black wooden box, there was a murmur of conversation among the villagers, and he waved and called. "Little late today, folks." The postmaster, Mr. Graves, followed him, carrying a three-legged stool, and the stool was put in the center of the square and Mr. Summers set the black box down on it. The villagers kept their distance, leaving a space between themselves and the stool, and when Mr. Summers said, "Some of you fellows want to give me a hand?" there was a hesitation before two men, Mr. Martin and his oldest son, Baxter, came forward to hold the box steady on the stool while Mr. Summers stirred up the papers inside it.

The original paraphernalia for the lottery had been lost long ago, and the black box now resting on the stool had been put into use even before Old Man Warner, the oldest man in town, was born. Mr. Summers spoke frequently to the villagers about making a new box, but no one liked to upset even as much tradition as was represented by the black box. There was a story that the present box had been made with some pieces of the box that had preceded it, the one that had been constructed when the first people settled down to make a village here. Every year, after the lottery, Mr. Summers began talking again about a new box, but every year the subject was allowed to fade off without anything's being done. The black box grew shabbier each year; by now it was no longer completely black but splintered badly along one side to show the original wood color, and in some places faded or stained.

Mr. Martin and his oldest son, Baxter, held the black box securely on the stool until Mr. Summers had stirred the papers thoroughly with his hand. Because so much of the ritual had been forgotten or discarded, Mr.

Summers had been successful in having slips of paper substituted for the chips of wood that had been used for generations. Chips of wood, Mr. Summers had argued, had been all very well when the village was tiny, but now that the population was more than three hundred and likely to keep on growing, it was necessary to use something that would fit more easily into he black box. The night before the lottery, Mr. Summers and Mr. Graves made up the slips of paper and put them in the box, and it was then taken to the safe of Mr. Summers' coal company and locked up until Mr. Summers was ready to take it to the square next morning. The rest of the year, the box was put way, sometimes one place, sometimes another; it had spent one year in Mr. Graves's barn and another year underfoot in the post office, and sometimes it was set on a shelf in the Martin grocery and left there.

There was a great deal of fussing to be done before Mr. Summers declared the lottery open. There were the lists to make up—of heads of families, heads of households in each family, members of each household in each family. There was the proper swearing-in of Mr. Summers by the postmaster, as the official of the lottery; at one time, some people remembered, there had been a recital of some sort, performed by the official of the lottery, a perfunctory, tuneless chant that had been rattled off duly each year; some people believed that the official of the lottery used to stand just so when he said or sang it, others believed that he was supposed to walk among the people, but years and years ago this part of the ritual had been allowed to lapse. There had been, also, a ritual salute, which the official of the lottery had had to use in addressing each person who came up to draw from the box, but this also had changed with time, until now it was felt necessary only for the official to speak to each person approaching. Mr. Summers was very good at all this; in his clean white shirt and blue jeans, with one hand resting carelessly on the black box, he seemed very proper and important as he talked interminably to Mr. Graves and the Martins.

Just as Mr. Summers finally left off talking and turned to the assembled villagers, Mrs. Hutchinson came hurriedly along the path to the square, her sweater thrown over her shoulders, and slid into place in the back of the crowd. "Clean forgot what day it was," she said to Mrs. Delacroix, who stood next to her, and they both laughed softly. "Thought my old man was out back stacking wood," Mrs. Hutchinson went on, "and then I looked out the window and the kids were gone, and then I remembered it was the twenty-seventh and came a-running." She dried her hands on her apron, and Mrs. Delacroix said, "You're in time, though. They're still talking away up there."

Mrs. Hutchinson craned her neck to see through the crowd and found her husband and children standing near the front. She tapped Mrs. Delacroix on the arm as a farewell and began to make her way through

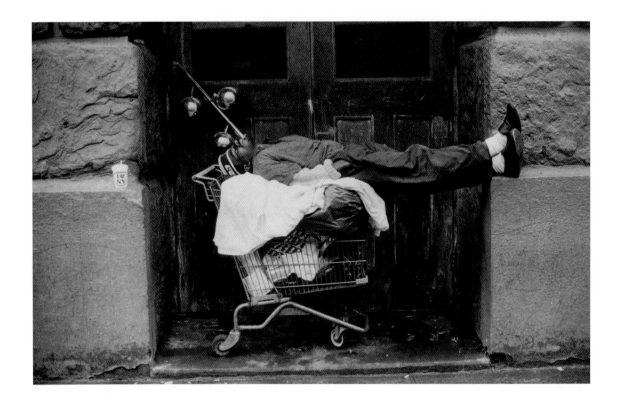

the crowd. The people separated good-humoredly to let her through; two or three people said, in voices just loud enough to be heard across the crowd, "Here comes your, Missus, Hutchinson," and "Bill, she made it after all." Mrs. Hutchinson reached her husband, and Mr. Summers, who had been waiting, said cheerfully, "Thought we were going to have to get on without you, Tessie." Mrs. Hutchinson said, grinning, "Wouldn't have me leave m'dishes in the sink, now, would you. Joe?" and soft laughter ran through the crowd as the people stirred back into position after Mrs. Hutchinson's arrival.

"Well, now," Mr. Summers said soberly, "guess we better get started, get this over with, so's we can go

Above: Andrew Lane, *Untitled*. Part of the power of this story is that, despite our determination to take control of our lives, there is always an element of lottery to life. How far is success or failure in American society a lottery?

back to work. Anybody ain't here?"

"Dunbar," several people said. "Dunbar, Dunbar."

Mr. Summers consulted his list. "Clyde Dunbar," he said. "That's right. He's broke his leg, hasn't he? Who's drawing for him?"

"Me, I guess," a woman said, and Mr. Summers turned to look at her. "Wife draws for her husband." Mr. Summers said. "Don't you have a grown boy to do it for you, Janey?" Although Mr. Summers and everyone else in the village knew the answer perfectly well, it was the business of the official of the lottery to ask such questions formally. Mr. Summers waited with an expression of polite interest while Mrs. Dunbar answered.

"Horace's not but sixteen yet." Mrs. Dunbar said regretfully. "Guess I gotta fill in for the old man this year."

"Right." Mr. Summers said. He made a note on the list he was holding. Then he asked, "Watson boy drawing this year?"

A tall boy in the crowd raised his hand. "Here," he said. "I'm drawing for my mother and me." He blinked his eyes nervously and ducked his head as several voices in the crowd said things like "Good fellow, Jack." and "Glad to see your mother's got a man to do it."

"Well," Mr. Summers said, "guess that's everyone. Old Man Warner make it?"

"Here," a voice said, and Mr. Summers nodded.

A sudden hush fell on the crowd as Mr. Summers cleared his throat and looked at the list. "All ready?" he called. "Now, I'll read the names—heads of families first—and the men come up and take a paper out of the box. Keep the paper folded in your hand without looking at it until everyone has had a turn. Everything clear?"

The people had done it so many times that they only half listened to the directions; most of them were quiet, wetting their lips, not looking around. Then Mr. Summers raised one hand high and said, "Adams." A man disengaged himself from the crowd and came forward. "Hi, Steve," Mr. Summers said, and Mr. Adams said, "Hi, Joe." They grinned at one another humorlessly and nervously. Then Mr. Adams reached into the black box and took out a folded paper. He held it firmly by one corner as he turned and went hastily back to his place in the crowd, where he stood a little apart from his family, not looking down at his hand.

"Allen," Mr. Summers said. "Anderson . . . . Bentham."

"Seems like there's no time at all between lotteries any more." Mrs. Delacroix said to Mrs. Graves in the back row.

"Seems like we got through with the last one only last week."

"Time sure goes fast," Mrs. Graves said.

"Clark . . . . Delacroix"

"There goes my old man," Mrs. Delacroix said. She held her breath while her husband went forward.

"Dunbar," Mr. Summers said, and Mrs. Dunbar went steadily to the box while one of the women said, "Go on, Janey," and another said, "There she goes."

"We're next." Mrs. Graves said. She watched while Mr. Graves came around from the side of the box, greeted Mr. Summers gravely, and selected a slip of paper from the box. By now, all through the crowd there were men holding the small folded papers in their large hands, turning them over and over nervously. Mrs. Dunbar and her two sons stood together, Mrs. Dunbar holding the slip of paper.

"Harburt . . . . Hutchinson."

"Get up there, Bill," Mrs. Hutchinson said, and the people near her laughed.

"Jones."

"They do say," Mr. Adams said to Old Man Warner, who stood next to him, "that over in the north village they're talking of giving up the lottery."

Old Man Warner snorted. "Pack of crazy fools," he said. "Listening to the young folks, nothing's good enough for *them*. Next thing you know, they'll be wanting to go back to living in caves, nobody work any more, live *that* way for a while. Used to be a saying about 'Lottery in June, corn be heavy soon.' First thing you know, we'd all be eating stewed chickweed and acorns. There's *always* been a lottery," he added petulantly. "Bad enough to see young Joe Summers up there joking with everybody."

"Some places have already quit lotteries," Mrs. Adams said.

"Nothing but trouble in *that*," Old Man Warner said stoutly. "Pack of young fools."

"Martin." And Bobby Martin watched his father go forward. "Overdyke . . . . Percy."

"I wish they'd hurry," Mrs. Dunbar said to her older son. "I wish they'd hurry."

"They're almost through," her son said.

"You get ready to run tell Dad," Mrs. Dunbar said.

Mr. Summers called his own name and then stepped forward precisely and selected a slip from the box. Then he called, "Warner."

"Seventy-seventh year I been in the lottery," Old Man Warner said as he went through the crowd.

"Seventy-seventh time."

"Watson," The tall boy came awkwardly through the crowd. Someone said, "Don't be nervous, Jack," and Mr. Summers said, "Take your time, son."

"Zanini."

After that, there was a long pause, a breathless pause, until Mr. Summers, holding his slip of paper in the air, said, "All right, fellows." For a minute, no one moved, and then all the slips of paper were opened. Suddenly, all the women began to speak at once, saying, "Who is it?" "Who's got it?" "Is it the Dunbars?" "Is it the Watsons?" Then the voices began to say, "It's Hutchinson. It's Bill," "Bill Hutchinson's got it."

"Go tell your father," Mrs. Dunbar said to her older son.

People began to look around to see the Hutchinsons. Bill Hutchinson was standing quiet, staring down at the paper in his hand. Suddenly, Tessie Hutchinson shouted to Mr. Summers, "You didn't give him time enough to take any paper he wanted. I saw you. It wasn't fair."

"Be a good sport, Tessie," Mrs. Delacroix called, and Mrs. Graves said, "All of us took the same chance."

"Shut up, Tessie," Bill Hutchinson said.

"Well, everyone," Mr. Summers said, "that was done pretty fast, and now we've got to be hurrying a little more to get done in time." He consulted his next list. "Bill," he said, "you draw for the Hutchinson family. You got any other households in the Hutchinsons."

"There's Don and Eva," Mrs. Hutchinson yelled. "Make *them* take their chance!"

"Daughters draw with their husbands' families, Tessie," Mr. Summers said gently. "You know that as well as anyone else."

"It wasn't *fair*," Tessie said.

We are all born whole and, let us hope, will die whole. But somewhere early on our way, we eat one of the wonderful fruits of the tree of knowledge, things separate into good and evil, and we begin the shadow-making process; we divide our lives. In the cultural process we sort out our God-given characteristics into those that are acceptable to our society and those that have to be put away. This is wonderful and necessary, and there would be no civilized behavior without this sorting out of good and evil. But the refused and unacceptable characteristics do not go away; they only collect in the dark corners of our personality. When they have been hidden long enough, they take on a life of their own—the shadow life.

——Robert A. Johnson

"I guess not, Joe," Bill Hutchinson said regretfully. "My daughter draws with her husband's family, that's only fair. And I've got no other family except the kids."

"Then, as far as drawing for families is concerned, it's you," Mr. Summers said in explanation, "and as far as drawing for households is concerned, that's you, too. Right?"

"Right," Bill Hutchinson said.

"How many kids, Bill?" Mr. Summers asked formally.

"Three," Bill Hutchinson said. "There's Bill, Jr., and Nancy, and little Dave. And Tessie and me."

"All right, then," Mr. Summers said. "Harry, you got their, tickets back?"

Mr. Graves nodded and held up the slips of paper. "Put them in the box, then," Mr. Summers directed. "Take Bill's and put it in."

"I think we ought to start over," Mrs. Hutchinson said, as quietly as she could. "I tell you it wasn't *fair*. You didn't give him time enough to choose. *Every*body saw that."

Mr. Graves had selected the five slips and put them in the box, and he dropped all the papers but those onto the ground, where the breeze caught them and lifted them off.

"Listen, everybody," Mrs. Hutchinson was saying to the people around her.

"Ready, Bill?" Mr. Summers asked, and Bill Hutchinson, with one quick glance around at his wife and children, nodded.

"Remember," Mr. Summers said, "take the slips and keep them folded until each person has taken one. Harry, you help little Dave." Mr. Graves took the hand of the little boy, who came willingly with him up to the box. "Take a paper out of the box, Davy." Mr. Summers said. Davy put his hand into the box and laughed. "Take just *one* paper." Mr. Summers said. "Harry, you hold it for him." Mr. Graves took the child's hand and removed the folded paper from the tight fist and held it while little Dave stood next to him and looked up at him wonderingly.

"Nancy next," Mr. Summers said. Nancy was twelve, and her school friends breathed heavily as she went forward switching her skirt, and took a slip daintily from the box. "Bill, Jr.," Mr. Summers said, and Billy, his face red and his feet over-large, near knocked the box over as he got a paper out. "Tessie," Mr. Summers said. She hesitated for a minute, looking around defiantly, and then set her lips and went up to the box. She snatched a paper out and held it behind her.

"Bill," Mr. Summers said, and Bill Hutchinson reached into the box and felt around, bringing his hand out at last with the slip of paper in it.

The crowd was quiet. A girl whispered, "I hope it's not Nancy," and the sound of the whisper reached the edges of the crowd.

"It's not the way it used to be." Old Man Warner said clearly. "People ain't the way they used to be."

"All right," Mr. Summers said. "Open the papers. Harry, you open little Dave's."

Mr. Graves opened the slip of paper and there was a general sigh through the crowd as he held it up and everyone could see that it was blank. Nancy and Bill, Jr., opened theirs at the same time, and both beamed and laughed, turning around to the crowd and holding their slips of paper above their heads.

"Tessie," Mr. Summers said. There was a pause, and then Mr. Summers looked at Bill Hutchinson, and Bill unfolded his paper and showed it. It was blank.

"It's Tessie," Mr. Summers said, and his voice was hushed. "Show us her paper, Bill."

Bill Hutchinson went over to his wife and forced the slip of paper out of her hand. It had a black spot on it, the black spot Mr. Summers had made the night before with the heavy pencil in the coal company office. Bill Hutchinson held it up, and there was a stir in the crowd.

"All right, folks," Mr. Summers said. "Let's finish quickly."

Although the villagers had forgotten the ritual and lost the original black box, they still remembered to use stones. The pile of stones the boys had made earlier was ready; there were stones on the ground with the blowing scraps of paper that had come out of the box. Delacroix selected a stone so large she had to pick it up with both hands and turned to Mrs. Dunbar. "Come on," she said. "Hurry up."

Mrs. Dunbar had small stones in both hands, and she said, gasping for breath. "I can't run at all. You'll have to go ahead and I'll catch up with you."

The children had stones already. And someone gave little Davy Hutchinson few pebbles.

Tessie Hutchinson was in the center of a cleared space by now, and she held her hands out desperately as the villagers moved in on her. "It isn't fair," she said. A stone hit her on the side of the head. Old Man Warner was saying, "Come on, come on, everyone." Steve Adams was in the front of the crowd of villagers, with Mrs. Graves beside him.

"It isn't fair, it isn't right," Mrs. Hutchinson screamed, and then they were upon her.

DIVING INTO THE WRECK

Adrienne Rich

First having read the book of myths,
and loaded the camera,
and checked the edge of the knife-blade,
I put on
the body-armor of black rubber
the absurd flippers
the grave and awkward mask.
I am having to do this
not like Cousteau with his
assiduous team
aboard the sun-flooded schooner
but here alone.

Left: Cathryn Chase, *Lookout.* This chilly, watery scene has a mythical dimension as does the poem.

There is a ladder.
The ladder is always there
hanging innocently
close to the side of the schooner.
We know what it is for,
we who have used it.
Otherwise
it's a piece of maritime floss
some sundry equipment.

I go down.
Rung after rung and still
the oxygen immerses me
the blue light
the clear atoms
of our human air.
I go down.
My flippers cripple me,
I crawl like an insect down the ladder
and there is no one
to tell me when the ocean
will begin.

First the air is blue and then
it is bluer and then green and then
black I am blacking out and yet
my mask is powerful
it pumps my blood with power
the sea is another story
the sea is not a question of power
I have to learn alone
to turn my body without force
in the deep element.

And now: it is easy to forget
what I came for
among so many who have always
lived here
swaying their crenelated fans
between the reefs
and besides
you breathe differently down here.

I came to explore the wreck.
The words are purposes.
The words are maps.
I came to see the damage that was done

and the treasures that prevail.
I stroke the beam of my lamp
slowly along the flank
of something more permanent
than fish or weed

the thing I came for:
the wreck and not the story of the wreck
the thing itself and not the myth
the drowned face always staring
toward the sun
the evidence of damage
worn by salt and sway into this threadbare beauty
the ribs of the disaster
curing their assertion
among the tentative haunters.

This is the place.
I am here, the mermaid whose dark hair
streams black, the merman in his armored body
We circle silently
about the wreck
we dive into the hold.
I am she: I am he

whose drowned face sleeps with open eyes
whose breasts still bear the stress
whose silver, copper, vermeil cargo lies
obscurely inside barrels
half-wedged and left to rot
we are the half-destroyed instruments
that once held to a course
the water-eaten log
the fouled compass

We are, I am, you are
by cowardice or courage
the one who find our way
back to this scene
carrying a knife, a camera
a book of myths
in which
our names do not appear.

YOUNG GOODMAN BROWN

Nathaniel Hawthorne

YOUNG GOODMAN BROWN CAME FORTH AT sunset, into the street at Salem village; but put his head back, after crossing the threshold, to exchange a parting kiss with his young wife. And Faith, as the wife was aptly named, thrust her own pretty head into the street, letting the wind play with the pink ribbons of her cap while she called to Goodman Brown.

"Dearest heart," whispered she, softly and rather sadly, when her lips were close to his ear, "prithee, put off your journey until sunrise, and sleep in your own bed tonight. A lone woman is troubled with such dreams and such thoughts that she's afeard of herself sometimes. Pray tarry with me this night, dear husband, of all nights in the year."

"My love and my Faith," replied young Goodman Brown, "of all nights in the year, this one night must I tarry away from thee. My journey, as thou callest it, forth and back again, must needs be done 'twixt now and sunrise. What, my sweet, pretty wife, dost thou doubt me already, and we but three months married!"

Right: Grant Wood, *American Gothic.* This is a famous image of the Puritan ethics and virtues still alive in American consciousness. The picture has also a sense of the sinister. The house behind them could almost be a church, the pitchfork could be seen as threatening, and the wife looks apprehensive. The artist, however, denied that he had depicted the intolerance and rigidity that can result from insular rural life, but felt that these Puritan values dignified the midwestern character.

"Then God bless you!" said Faith, with the pink ribbons; "and may you find all well, when you come back."

"Amen!" cried Goodman Brown. "Say thy prayers, dear Faith, and go to bed at dusk, and no harm will come to thee."

So they parted; and the young man pursued his way until, being about to turn the corner by the meeting-house, he looked back and saw the head of Faith still peeping after him, with a melancholy air, in spite of her pink ribbons.

Above: Andrew Lane, *Untitled.*

"Poor little Faith!" thought he, for his heart smote him. "What a wretch am I to leave her on such an errand! She talks of dreams, too. Methought as she spoke there was trouble in her face, as if a dream had warned her what work is to be done tonight. But, no, no; 't would kill her to think it. Well; she's a blessed angel on earth; and after this one night, I'll cling to her skirts and follow her to heaven."

With this excellent resolve for the future, Goodman Brown felt himself justified in making more haste on his present evil purpose. He had taken a dreary road, darkened by all the gloomiest trees of the forest, which barely stood aside to let the narrow path creep through, and closed immediately behind. It was all as lonely as could be; and there is this peculiarity in such a solitude, that the traveler knows not who may be concealed by the innumerable trunks and the thick boughs overhead; so that with lonely footsteps he may yet be passing through an unseen multitude.

"There may be a devilish Indian behind every tree," said Goodman Brown to himself; and he glanced fearfully behind him as he added, "What if the devil himself should be at my very elbow!"

His head being turned back, he passed a crook of the road, and, looking forward again, beheld the figure of a man, in grave and decent attire, seated at the foot of an old tree. He arose at Goodman Brown's approach and walked onward side by side with him.

"You are late, Goodman Brown," said he. "The clock of the Old South was striking as I came through Boston and that is full fifteen minutes agone."

"Faith kept me back awhile," replied the young man, with a tremor in his voice, caused by the sudden appearance of his companion, though not wholly unexpected.

It was now deep dusk in the forest, and deepest in that part of it where these two were journeying. As nearly as could be discerned, the second traveler was about fifty years old, apparently in the same rank of life as Goodman Brown, and bearing a considerable resemblance to him, though perhaps more in expression than features. Still, they might have been taken for father and son. And yet, though the elder person was as simply clad as the younger, and as simple in manner too, he had an indescribable air of one who knew the world, and would not have felt abashed at the governor's dinner table or in King William's court, were it possible that his affairs should call him thither. But the only thing about him that could be fixed upon as remarkable was his staff, which bore the likeness of a great black snake, so curiously wrought that it might almost be seen to twist and wriggle itself like a living serpent. This, of course, must have been an ocular deception, assisted by the uncertain light.

"Come, Goodman Brown!" cried his fellow-traveler, "this is a dull pace for the beginning of a journey. Take my staff, if you are so soon weary.

"Friend," said the other, exchanging his slow pace for a full stop, "having kept covenant by meeting thee here, it is my purpose now to return whence I came. I have scruples, touching the matter thou wot'st of."

"Sayest thou so?" replied he of the serpent, smiling apart. "Let us walk on, nevertheless, reasoning as we go and if I convince thee not thou shalt turn back. We are but a little way in the forest yet."

"Too far, too far!" exclaimed the goodman, unconsciously resuming his walk. "My father never went into the woods on such an errand, nor his father before him. We have been a race of honest men and good Christians, since the days of the martyrs; and shall I be the first of the name of Brown that ever took this path and kept—"

"Such company, thou wouldst say," observed the elder person, interpreting his pause. "Well said, Goodman Brown! I have been as well acquainted with your family as with ever a one among the Puritans; and that's no trifle to say. I helped your grandfather, the constable, when he lashed the Quaker woman so smartly through the streets of Salem; and it was I that brought your father a pitch-pine knot, kindled at my own hearth, to set fire to an Indian village, in King Philip's War. They were my good friends, both; and many a pleasant walk have we had along this path, and returned merrily after midnight. I would fain be friends with you for their sake."

"If it be as thou sayest," replied Goodman Brown, "I marvel they never spoke of these matters. Or, verily, I marvel not, seeing that the least rumor of the sort would have driven them from New England. We are a people of prayer, and good works to boot, and abide no such wickedness."

"Wickedness or not," said the traveler with the twisted staff, have a very general acquaintance here in New England. The deacons of many a church have drunk the communion wine with me; the selectmen, of divers towns make me their chairman; and a majority of the Great and General Court are firm supporters of my interest. The governor and I, too—but these are state secrets."

"Can this be so" cried Goodman Brown, with a stare of amazement at his undisturbed companion. "Howbeit, I have nothing to do with the governor and council; they have their own ways, and are no rule for a simple husbandman like me. But, were I to go on with thee, how should I meet the eye of that good old man, our minister, at Salem village? Oh, his voice would make me tremble both Sabbath day and lecture day!"

Thus far the elder traveler had listened with due gravity; but now burst into a fit of irrepressible mirth, shaking himself so violently that his snake-like staff actually seemed to wriggle in sympathy.

"Ha! ha! ha!" shouted he again and again; then composing himself, "Well, go on, Goodman Brown, go on; but, prithee, don't kill me with laughing!"

"Well, then, to end the matter at once," said Goodman Brown, considerably nettled, "there is my wife, Faith. It would break her dear little heart; and I'd rather break my own."

"Nay, if that be the case," answered the other, "e'en go thy ways, Goodman Brown. I would not for twenty old women like the one hobbling before us that Faith should come to any harm."

As he spoke, he pointed his staff at a female figure on the path, in whom Goodman Brown recognized a very pious and exemplary dame, who had taught him his catechism in youth, and was still his moral and spiritual adviser, jointly with the minister and Deacon Gookin.

"A marvel, truly, that Goody Cloyse should be so far in the wilderness, at nightfall!" said he. "But with your leave, friend, I shall take a cut through the woods until we have left this Christian woman behind. Being a stranger to you, she might ask whom I was consorting with and whither I was going."

"Be it so," said his fellow-traveler. "Betake you to the woods, and let me keep the path."

Accordingly, the young man turned aside, but took care to watch his companion, who advanced softly along the road until he had come within a staff's length of the old dame. She, meanwhile, was making the best of her way, with singular speed for so aged a woman, and mumbling some indistinct words—a prayer, doubtless—as she went. The traveler put forth his staff, and touched her withered neck with what seemed the serpent's tail.

"The devil!" screamed the pious old lady.

"Then Goody Cloyse knows her old friend?" observed the traveler, confronting her and leaning on his writhing stick.

"Ah, forsooth, and is it your worship indeed?" cried the good dame. "Yea, truly is it, and in the very image of my old gossip, Goodman Brown, the grandfather of the silly fellow that now is. But—would your worship believe it?—my broomstick hath strangely disappeared, stolen, as I suspect, by that unhanged witch, Goody Cory, and that, too, when I was all anointed with the juice of smallage and cinquefoil and wolf's bane—"

"Mingled with fine wheat and the fat of a new-born babe," said the shape of old Goodman Brown.

"Ah, your worship knows the recipe," cried the old lady, cackling aloud. "So, as I was saying, being all ready for the meeting, and no horse to ride on, I made up my mind to foot it; for they tell me, there is a nice young man to be taken into communion tonight. But now your good worship will lend me your arm, and we shall be there in a twinkling."

"That can hardly be," answered her friend. "I may not spare you my arm, Goody Cloyse, but here is my staff, if you will."

So saying, he threw it down at her feet, where, perhaps, it assumed life, being one of the rods which its owner had formerly lent to the Egyptian Magi. Of this fact, however, Goodman Brown could not take cognizance. He had cast up his eyes in astonishment, and, looking down again beheld neither Goody Cloyse nor the serpentine staff, but this fellow-traveler alone, who waited for him as calmly as if nothing had happened.

"That old woman taught me my catechism," said the young man; and there was a world of meaning in this simple comment.

They continued to walk onward, while the elder traveler exhorted his companion to make good speed and persevere in the path, discoursing so aptly that his arguments seemed rather to spring up in the bosom of his auditor than to be suggested by himself. As they went, he plucked a branch of maple to serve for a walking-stick, and began to strip it of the twigs and little boughs, which were wet with evening dew. The moment his fingers touched them they became strangely withered and dried up as with a week's sunshine. Thus the pair proceeded, at a good free pace, until suddenly, in a gloomy hollow of the road, Goodman Brown sat himself down on the stump of a tree and refused to go any farther.

"Friend," said he, stubbornly, "my mind is made up. Not another step will I budge on this errand. What if a wretched old woman do choose to go to the devil when I thought she was going to heaven: Is that any reason why I should quit my dear Faith and go after her?"

"You will think better of this by and by," said his acquaintance, composedly. "Sit here and rest yourself a while; and when you feel like moving again, there is my staff to help you along."

Without more words, he threw his companion the maple stick, and was as speedily out of sight as if he had vanished into the deepening gloom. The young man sat a few moments by the roadside, applauding himself greatly, and thinking with how clear a conscience he should meet the minister in his morning-walk, nor shrink from the eye of good old Deacon Gookin. And what calm sleep would be his that very night, which was to have been spent so wickedly, but purely and sweetly now, in the arms of Faith! Amidst these pleasant and praiseworthy meditations, Goodman Brown heard the tramp of horses along the road, and deemed it advisable to conceal himself within the verge of the forest, conscious of the guilty purpose that had brought him thither, though now so happily turned from it.

On came the hoof tramps and the voices of the riders, two grave old voices, conversing soberly as they drew near. These mingled sounds appeared to pass along the road, within a few yards of the young man's hiding-place; but, owing doubtless to the depth of the gloom at that particular spot, neither the travelers nor their steeds were visible. Though their figures brushed the small boughs by the wayside, it could not be seen that they intercepted, even for a moment, the faint gleam from the strip of bright sky athwart which they must have passed. Goodman Brown alternately crouched and stood on tip-toe, pulling aside the branches and thrusting forth his head as far as he durst without discerning so much as a shadow. It vexed him the more, because he could have sworn, were such a thing possible, that he recognized the voices of the minister and Deacon Gookin, jogging along quietly, as they were wont to do, when bound to some ordination or ecclesiastical council. While yet within hearing, one of the riders stopped to pluck a switch.

"Of the two, reverend sir," said the voice like the deacon's, "I had rather miss an ordination dinner than tonight's meeting. They tell me that some of our community are to be here from Falmouth and beyond, and others from Connecticut and Rhode Island; besides several of the Indian powows, who, after their fashion, know almost as much deviltry as the best of us. Moreover, there is a goodly young woman to be taken into communion."

"Mighty well, Deacon Gookin!" replied the solemn old tones of the minister. "Spur up, or we shall be late. Nothing can be done, you know, until I get on the ground."

The hoofs clattered again; and the voices, talking so strangely in the empty air, passed on through the forest, where no church had ever been gathered nor solitary Christian prayed. Whither, then, could these holy men be journeying so deep into the heathen wilderness? Young Goodman Brown caught hold of a tree for support, being ready to sink down on the ground, faint and overburdened with the heavy sickness of his heart. He looked up to the sky, doubting whether there really was a Heaven above him. Yet there was the blue arch, and the stars brightening in it.

"With heaven above and Faith below, I will yet stand firm against the devil!" cried Goodman Brown.

While he still gazed upward into the deep arch of the firmament and had lifted his hands to pray, a cloud, though no wind was stirring, hurried across the zenith and hid the brightening stars. The blue sky was still visible, except directly overhead, where this black mass of cloud was sweeping swiftly northward. Aloft in the air, as if from the depths of the cloud, came a confused and doubtful sound of voices. Once the listener fancied that he could distinguish the accent of townspeople of his own, men and women, both pious and ungodly, many of whom he had met at the communion table, and had seen others rioting at the tavern. The next moment, so indistinct were the sounds, he doubted whether he had heard aught but the murmur of the old forest, whispering without a wind. Then came a stronger swell of those familiar tones, heard daily in the sunshine at Salem village, but never until now from a cloud of night. There was one voice, of a young woman, uttering lamentations, yet with an uncertain sorrow, and entreating for some favor, which, perhaps, it would grieve her to obtain; and all the unseen multitude, both saints and sinners, seemed to encourage her onward.

"Faith!" shouted Goodman Brown, in a voice of agony and desperation; and the echoes of the forest mocked him, crying, "Faith! Faith!" as if bewildered wretches were seeking her, all through the wilderness.

The cry of grief, rage, and terror, was yet piercing the night, when the unhappy husband held his breath for a response. There was a scream, drowned immediately in a louder murmur of voices, fading into far-off laughter, as the dark cloud swept away, leaving the clear and silent sky above Goodman Brown. But something fluttered lightly down through the air, and caught on the branch of a tree. The young man seized it, and beheld a pink ribbon.

"My Faith is gone!" cried he, after one stupefied moment. "There is no good on earth; and sin is but a name. Come, devil! for to thee is this world given."

And, maddened with despair, so that he laughed loud and long, did Goodman Brown grasp his staff and set forth again, at such a rate that he seemed to fly along the forest path, rather than to walk or run. The road grew wilder and drearier and more faintly traced, and vanished at length, leaving him in the heart of the dark wilderness, still rushing onward with the instinct that guides mortal man to evil. The whole forest was peopled with frightful sounds—the creaking of the trees, the howling of wild beasts, and the yell of Indians; while sometimes the wind tolled like a distant church bell, and sometimes gave a broad roar around the traveler, as if all Nature were laughing him to scorn. But he was himself the chief horror of the scene, and shrank not from its other horrors.

"Ha! ha! ha!" roared Goodman Brown when the wind laughed at him. "Let us hear which will laugh loudest. Think not to frighten me with your deviltry. Come witch, come wizard, come Indian powwow, come devil himself, and here comes Goodman Brown. You may as well fear him as he fear you."

In truth, all through the haunted forest there could be nothing more frightful than the figure of Goodman Brown. On he flew, among the black pines, brandishing his staff with frenzied gestures, now giving vent to an inspiration of horrid blasphemy, and now shouting forth such laughter as set all the echoes of the forest laughing like demons around him. The fiend in his own shape is less hideous than when he rages in the breast of man. Thus sped the demoniac on his course, until, quivering among the trees, he saw a red light before him, as when the felled trunks and branches of a clearing have been set on fire, and throw up their lurid blaze against the sky, at the hour of midnight. He paused, in a lull of the tempest that had driven him onward, and heard the swell of what seemed a hymn, rolling solemnly from a distance with the weight of many voices. He knew the tune; it was a familiar one in the choir of the village meeting house. The verse died heavily away, and was lengthened by a chorus, not of human voices, but of all the sounds of the benighted wilderness pealing in awful harmony together. Goodman Brown cried out, and his cry was lost to his own ear by its unison with the cry of the desert.

In the interval of silence he stole forward until the light glared full upon his eyes. At one extremity of an open space, hemmed in by the dark wall of the forest, arose a rock, bearing some rude, natural resemblance either to an altar or a pulpit, and surrounded by four blazing pines, their tops aflame, their stems untouched, like candles at an evening meeting. The mass of foliage that had overgrown the summit of the rock was all on fire, blazing high into the night and fitfully illuminating the whole field. Each pendant twig and leafy festoon was in a blaze. As the red light arose and fell, a numerous congregation alternately shone forth, then disappeared in shadow, and again grew, as it were, out of the darkness, peopling the heart of the solitary woods at once.

"A grave and dark-clad company." quoth Goodman Brown.

In truth they were such. Among them, quivering to and fro between gloom and splendor, appeared faces that would be seen next day at the council board of the province, and others which, Sabbath after Sabbath, looked devoutly heavenward, and benignantly over the crowded pews, from the holiest pulpits in the land. Some affirm that the lady of the governor was there. At least there were high dames well known to her, and wives of honored husbands, and widows, a great multitude, and ancient maidens, all of excellent repute, and fair young girls, who trembled lest their mothers should espy them. Either the sudden gleams of light flashing over the obscure field bedazzled Goodman Brown, or he recognized a score of the church members of Salem village famous for their especial sanctity. Good old Deacon Gookin had arrived, and waited at the skirts of that venerable saint, his reverend pastor. But, irreverently consorting with these grave, reputable, and pious people, these elders of the church, these chaste dames and dewy virgins, there were men of dissolute lives and women of spotted fame, wretches given over to all mean and filthy vice, and suspected even of horrid crimes. It was strange to see that the good shrank not from the wicked, nor were the sinners abashed by the saints. Scattered also among their pale-faced enemies were the Indian priests, or powwows, who had often scared their native forest with more hideous incantations than any known to English witchcraft.

"But where is Faith?" thought Goodman Brown; and, as hope came into his heart, he trembled.

Another verse of the hymn arose, a slow and mournful strain, such as the pious love, but joined to words which expressed all that our nature can conceive of sin, and darkly hinted at far more. Unfathomable to mere mortals is the lore of fiends. Verse after verse was sung; and still the chorus of the desert swelled between like the deepest tone of a mighty organ; and with the final peal of that dreadful anthem there came a sound, as if the roaring wind, the rushing streams, the howling beasts, and every other voice of the unconverted wilderness were mingling and according with the voice of guilty man in homage to the prince of all. The four blazing pines threw up a loftier flame, and obscurely discovered shapes and visages of horror on the smoke wreaths above the impious assembly. At the same moment the fire on the rock shot redly forth and formed a glowing arch above its base, where now appeared a figure. With reverence be it spoken, the apparition bore no slight similitude, both in garb and manner, to some grave divine of the New England churches.

"Bring forth the converts!" cried a voice that echoed through the field and rolled into the forest.

At the word, Goodman Brown stepped forth from the shadow of the trees and approached the congregation, with whom he felt a loathful brotherhood by the sympathy of all that was wicked in his heart. He could have well nigh sworn that the shape of his own dead father beckoned him to advance, looking downward from a smoke wreath, while a woman, with dim features of despair, threw out her hand to warn him back. Was it his mother? But he had no power to retreat one step, nor to resist, even in thought, when the minister and good old Deacon Gookin seized his arms and led him to the blazing rock. Thither came also the slender form of a veiled female, led between Goody Cloyse, that pious teacher of the catechism, and Martha Carrier, who had received the devil's promise to be queen of hell. A rampant hag was she. And there stood the proselytes beneath the canopy of fire.

"Welcome, my children," said the dark figure, "to the communion of your race. Ye have found thus young your nature and your destiny. My children, look behind you!"

They turned; and flashing forth, as it were, in a sheet of flame, the fiend worshippers were seen; the smile of welcome gleamed darkly on every visage.

"There," resumed the sable form, "are all whom ye have reverenced from youth. Ye deemed them holier than yourselves, and shrank from your own sin, contrasting it with their lives of righteousness and prayerful aspirations heavenward. Yet here are they all in my worshipping assembly. This night it shall be granted you to know their secret deeds; how hoary-bearded elders of the church have whispered wanton words to the young maids of their households; how many a woman, eager for widows' weeds, has given her husband a drink at bedtime and let him sleep his last sleep in her bosom; how beardless youth have made haste to inherit their fathers' wealth; and how fair damsels—blush not, sweet ones—have dug little graves in the garden, and bidden me, the sole guest, to an infant's funeral. By the sympathy of your human hearts for sin ye shall scent out all the places—whether in church, bed-chamber, street, field, or forest—where crime has been committed, and shall exult to behold the whole earth one stain of guilt, one mighty bloodspot. Far more than this. It shall be yours to penetrate, in every bosom, the deep mystery of sin, the fountain of all wicked arts, and which inexhaustibly supplies more evil impulses than human power—than my power at its utmost—can make manifest in deeds. And now, my children, look upon each other."

They did so; and, by the blaze of the hell-kindled torches, the wretched man beheld his Faith, and the wife her husband, trembling before that unhallowed altar.

"Lo! there ye stand, my children," said the figure, in a deep and solemn tone, almost sad with its despairing awfulness, as if his once angelic nature could yet mourn for our miserable race. "Depending upon one another's hearts, ye had still hoped that virtue were not all a dream. Now are ye undeceived! Evil is the nature of mankind. Evil must be your only happiness. Welcome again, my children, to the communion of your race."

"Welcome." repeated the fiend worshippers, in one cry of despair and triumph.

And there they stood, the only pair, as it seemed, who were yet hesitating on the verge of wickedness in this dark world. A basin was hollowed, naturally, in a rock. Did it contain water, reddened by the lurid light? or was it blood? or, perchance, a liquid flame? Herein did the shape of evil dip his hand, and prepare to lay the mark of baptism upon their foreheads, that they might be partakers of the mystery of sin, more conscious of the secret guilt of others, both in deed and thought, than they could now be of their own. The husband cast one look at his pale wife, and Faith at him. What polluted wretches would the next glance show them to each other, shuddering alike at what they disclosed and what they saw!

"Faith! Faith!" cried the husband, "look up to heaven, and resist the wicked one!"

Whether Faith obeyed he knew not. Hardly had he spoken when he

If we repress the shadow we are only half people. That's why there are in literature tales about the devil who steals the shadow from people. Then they are...in the claws of the devil. We need a shadow. The shadow keeps us down to earth, reminds us of our incompleteness, and provides us with complementary traits. We would be very poor indeed if we were only what we imagined ourselves to be.

——Maria von Franz

found himself amid calm night and solitude, listening to a roar of the wind which died heavily away through the forest. He staggered against the rock, and felt it chill and damp; while a hanging twig, that had been all on fire, besprinkled his cheek with the coldest dew.

The next morning, young Goodman Brown came slowly into the street of Salem village, staring around him like a bewildered man. The good old minister was taking a walk along the graveyard to get an appetite for breakfast and meditate his sermon, and bestowed a blessing, as he passed, on Goodman Brown. He shrank from the venerable saint as if to avoid an anathema. Old Deacon Gookin was at domestic worship, and the holy words of his prayer were heard through the open window. "What God doth the wizard pray to?" quoth Goodman Brown. Goody Cloyse, that excellent old Christian, stood in the early sunshine, at her own lattice, catechising a little girl who had brought her a pint of morning's milk. Goodman Brown snatched away the child as from the grasp of the fiend himself. Turning the corner by the meeting-house, he spied the head of Faith, with the pink ribbons, gazing anxiously forth, and bursting into such joy at sight of him that she skipped along the street and almost kissed her husband before the whole village. But Goodman Brown looked sternly and sadly into her face, and passed on without a greeting.

Had Goodman Brown fallen asleep in the forest and only dreamed a wild dream of a witch-meeting?

Be it so, if you will; but, alas! it was a dream of evil omen for young Goodman Brown. A stern, a sad, a darkly meditative, a distrustful, if not a desperate man did he become from the night of that fearful dream. On the Sabbath day, when the congregation were singing a holy psalm, he could not listen because an anthem of sin rushed loudly upon his ear and drowned all the blessed strain. When the minister spoke from the pulpit with power and fervid eloquence, and, with his hand on the open Bible, of the sacred truths of our religion, and of saint-like lives and triumphant deaths, and of future bliss or misery unutterable, then did Goodman Brown turn pale, dreading lest the roof should thunder down upon the gray blasphemer and his hearers. Often, awaking suddenly at midnight, he shrank from the bosom of Faith; and at morning or eventide, when the family knelt down at prayer, he scowled and muttered to himself, and gazed sternly at his wife, and turned away. And when he had lived long, and was borne to his grave a hoary corpse, followed by Faith, an aged woman, and children and grandchildren, a goodly procession, besides neighbors not a few, they carved no hopeful verse upon his tombstone, for his dying hour was gloom.

NOT WITH A BANG

Howard Fast

O N THE EVENING OF THE THIRD OF APRIL, STANDING AT THE WINDOW OF HIS pleasant three-bedroom, split-level house and admiring the sunset, Alfred Collins saw a hand rise above the horizon, spread thumb and forefinger, and snuff out the sun. It was the moment of soft twilight, and it ended as abruptly as if someone had flicked an electric switch.

Which is precisely what his wife did. She put on lights all over the house. "My goodness, Al," she said, "it did get dark quickly, didn't it?"

"That's because someone snuffed out the sun."

"What on earth are you talking about?" she asked. "And by the way, the Bensons are coming for dinner and bridge tonight, so you'd better get dressed."

"All right. You weren't watching the sunset, were you?"

"I have other things to do."

"Yes. Well, what I mean is that if you were watching, you would have seen this hand come up behind the horizon, and then the thumb and forefinger just spread out, and then they came together and snuffed out the sun."

Left: Cathryn Chase, *Gate.*

"Really. Now for heaven's sake, Al, don't redouble tonight. If you are doubled, have faith in your bad bidding. Do you promise me?"

"Funniest damn thing about the hand. It brought back all my childhood memories of anthropomorphism."

"And just what does that mean?"

"Nothing. Nothing at all. I'm going to take a shower."

"Don't be all evening about it."

At dinner, Al Collins asked Steve Benson whether he had been watching the sunset that evening.

"No-no, I was showering."

"And you, Sophie?" Collins asked of Benson's wife.

"No way. I was changing a hem. What does women's lib intend to do about hems? There's the essence of the status of women, the nitty-gritty of our servitude."

"It's one of Al's jokes," Mrs. Collins explained. "He was standing at the window and he saw this hand come over the horizon and snuff out the sun."

"Did you, Al?"

"Scout's honor. The thumb and forefinger parted, then came together. Poof. Out went the sun."

"That's absolutely delicious," Sophie said. "You have such delicious imagination."

"Especially in his bidding," his wife remarked.

"She'll never forget that slam bid doubled and redoubled," Sophie said. It was evident that she would never forget it either.

"Interesting but impractical," said Steve Benson, who was an engineer at IBM. "You're dealing with a body that is almost a million miles in diameter. The internal temperature is over ten million degrees centigrade, and at its core the hydrogen atoms are reduced to helium ash. So all you have is poetic symbolism. The sun will be here for a long time."

After the second rubber, Sophie Benson remarked that either it was chilly in the Collins house or she was catching something.

"Al, turn up the thermostat," said Mrs. Collins.

The Collins team won the third and fourth rubbers, and Mrs. Collins had all the calm superiority of a winner as she bid her guests good night. Al Collins went out to the car with them, thinking that, after all, suburban living was a strange process of isolation and alienation. In the city, a million people must have watched the thing happen; here, Steve Benson was taking a shower and his wife was changing a hem.

It was a very cold night for April. Puddles of water left over from a recent rain had frozen solid, and the star-drenched sky had the icy look of midwinter. Both of the Bensons had arrived without coats, and as they hurried into their car, Benson laughingly remarked that AI was probably right about the sun. Benson had difficulty starting the car, and AI Collins stood shivering until they had driven away. Then he looked at the outside thermometer. It was down to sixteen degrees.

"Well, we beat them loud and clear," his wife observed when he came back to the house. He helped her clean up, and while they were at it, she asked him just what he meant by anthropomorphism or whatever it was.

"It's sort of a primitive notion. You know, the Bible says that God made man in His own image."

"Oh? You know, I absolutely believed it when I was a child. What are you doing?"

He was at the fireplace, and he said that he thought he'd build a fire.

"In April? You must be out of your mind. Anyway, I cleaned the hearth."

"I'll clean it up tomorrow."

"Well, I'm going to bed. I think you're crazy to start a fire at this time of the night, but I'm not going to argue with you. This is the first time you did not overbid, and thank heavens for small favors."

The wood was dry, and the fire was warm and pleasant to watch. Collins had never lost his pleasure at watching the flames of a fire, and he mixed himself a long scotch and water, and sat in front of the flames, sipping the drink and recalling his own small scientific knowledge. The green plants would die within a week, and after that the oxygen would go. How long? he wondered. Two days—ten days—he couldn't remember and he had no inclination to go to the encyclopedia and find out. It would get very cold, terribly cold. It surprised him that instead of being afraid, he was only mildly curious.

He looked at the thermometer again before he went to bed. It was down to zero now. In the bedroom, his wife was already asleep, and he undressed quietly and put an extra comforter on the bed before he crawled in next to her. She moved toward him, and feeling her warm body next to him, he fell asleep.

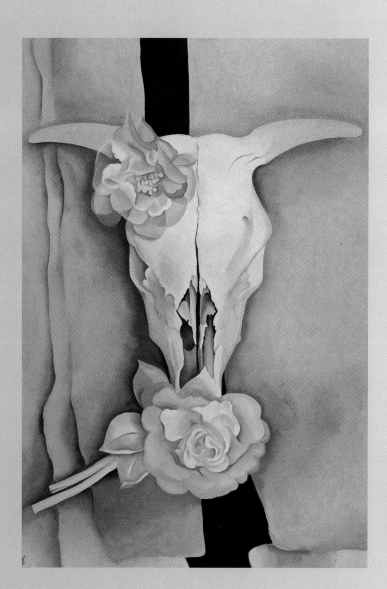

Left: Georgia O'Keeffe, *Cow's Skull with Calico Roses.* Georgia O'Keeffe collected sun-bleached bones from the desert around her home and used them often in her art. Although bones are usually symbolic of death, the sensuality of her paintings has imbued them with life, and they echo the poem's theme of death and immortality.

IN A DISUSED GRAVEYARD

Robert Frost

THE LIVING COME WITH GRASSY TREAD
To read the gravestones on the hill;
The graveyard draws the living still,
But never anymore the dead.
The verses in it say and say:
"The ones who living come today
To read the stones and go away
Tomorrow dead will come to stay."
So sure of death the marbles rhyme,
Yet can't help marking all the time
How no one dead will seem to come.
What is it men are shrinking from?
It would be easy to be clever
And tell the stones: Men hate to die
And have stopped dying now forever.
I think they would believe the lie.

SUNDAY IN THE PARK

Bel Kaufman

I T WAS STILL WARM IN THE LATE-afternoon sun, and the city noises came muffled through the trees in the park. She put her book down on the bench, removed her sunglasses, and sighed contentedly. Morton was reading the *Times Magazine* section, one arm flung around her shoulder; their three-year-old son, Larry, was playing in the sandbox: a faint breeze fanned

Left: A confrontation between police and anti-Vietnam protestors in 1968. At the height of the student protests, there was a belief that such violence was justified. In the accompanying story, the uncomfortable question arises of how far should the man have gone in defence of his family—should he, in fact, have risked violence?

her hair softly against her cheek. It was five-thirty of a Sunday afternoon, and the small playground, tucked away in a corner of the park, was all but deserted. The swings and seesaws stood motionless and abandoned, the slides were empty, and only in the sandbox two little boys squatted diligently side by side. *How good this is*, she thought, and almost smiled at her sense of well-being. They must go out in the sun more often; Morton was so city-pale, cooped up all week inside the gray factorylike university. She squeezed his arm affectionately and glanced at Larry, delighting in the pointed little face frowning in concentration over the tunnel he was digging. The other boy suddenly stood up and with a quick, deliberate swing of his chubby arm threw a spadeful of sand at Larry. It just missed his head. Larry continued digging; the boy remained standing, shovel raised, stolid and impassive.

    "No, no, little boy." She shook her finger at him, her eyes searching for the child's mother or nurse. "We mustn't throw sand. It may get in someone's eyes and hurt. We must play nicely in the nice sandbox." The boy looked at her in unblinking expectancy. He was about Larry's age but perhaps ten pounds heavier, a husky little boy with none of Larry's quickness and sensitivity in his face. Where was his mother? The only other people left in the playground were two women and a little girl on roller skates leaving now through the gate, and a man on a bench a few feet away. He was a big man, and he seemed to be taking up the whole bench as he held the Sunday comics close to his face. She supposed he was the child's father. He did not look up from his comics, but spat once deftly out of the corner of his mouth. She turned her eyes away.

    At that moment, as swiftly as before, the fat little boy threw another spadeful of sand at Larry. This time some of it landed on his hair and forehead. Larry looked up at his mother, his mouth tentative; her expression would tell him whether to cry or not.

    Her first instinct was to rush to her son, brush the sand out of his hair, and punish the other child, but she controlled it. She always said that she wanted Larry to learn to fight his own battles.

"Don't *do* that, little boy," she said sharply, leaning forward on the bench. "You mustn't throw sand!"

The man on the bench moved his mouth as if to spit again, but instead he spoke. He did not look at her, but at the boy only.

"You go right ahead, Joe," he said loudly. "Throw all you want. This here is a *public* sandbox."

She felt a sudden weakness in her knees as she glanced at Morton. He had become aware of what was happening. He put his *Times* down carefully on his lap and turned his fine, lean face toward the man, smiling the shy, apologetic smile he might have offered a student in pointing out an error in his thinking. When he spoke to the man, it was with his usual reasonableness.

"You're quite right," he said pleasantly, "but just because this is a public place. . . ."

The man lowered his funnies and looked at Morton. He looked at him from head to foot, slowly and deliberately. "Yeah?" His insolent voice was edged with menace. "My kid's got just as good right here as yours, and if he feels like throwing sand, he'll throw it, and if you don't like it, you can take your kid the hell out of here."

The children were listening, their eyes and mouths wide open, their spades forgotten in small fists. She noticed the muscle in Morton's jaw tighten. He was rarely angry; he seldom lost his temper. She was suffused with a tenderness for her husband and an impotent rage against the man for involving him in a situation so alien and so distasteful to him.

"Now, just a minute," Morton said courteously, "you must realize. . . ."

"Aw, shut up," said the man.

Her heart began to pound. Morton half rose; the *Times* slid to the ground. Slowly the other man stood up. He took a couple of steps toward Morton, then stopped. He flexed his great arms, waiting. She pressed her trembling knees together. Would there be violence, fighting? How dreadful, how incredible. . . . She must do something, stop them, call for help. She wanted to put her hand on her husband's sleeve, to pull him down, but for some reason she didn't.

Morton adjusted his glasses. He was very pale. "This is ridiculous," he said unevenly. "I must ask you. . . ."

"Oh, yeah?" said the man. He stood with his legs spread apart, rocking a little, looking at Morton with utter scorn. "You and who else?"

For a moment the two men looked at each other nakedly. Then Morton turned his back on the man and said quietly, "Come on, let's get out of here." He walked awkwardly, almost limping with self-consciousness, to the sandbox. He stooped and lifted Larry and his shovel out.

At once Larry came to life; his face lost its rapt expression and he began to kick and cry. "I don't *want* to go home, I want to play better, I don't *want* any supper, I don't *like* supper. . . ." It became a chant as they walked, pulling their child between them, his feet dragging on the ground. In order to get to the exit gate they had to pass the bench where the man sat sprawling again. She was careful not to look at him. With all the dignity she could summon, she pulled Larry's sandy, perspiring little hand, while Morton pulled the other. Slowly and with head high she walked with her husband and child out of the playground.

Her first feelings was one of relief that a fight had been avoided, that no one was hurt. Yet beneath it there was a layer of something else, something heavy and inescapable. She sensed that it was more than just an unpleasant incident, more than defeat of reason by force. She felt dimly it had something to do with her and Morton, something acutely personal, familiar, and important.

Suddenly Morton spoke. "It wouldn't have proved anything."

"What?" she asked.

"A fight. It wouldn't have proved anything beyond the fact that he's bigger than I am."

"Of course," she said

"The only possible outcome," he continued reasonably, "would have been—what? My glasses broken, perhaps a tooth or two replaced, a couple of days' work missed—and for what? For justice? For truth?"

"Of course," she repeated. She quickened her step. She wanted only to get home and to busy herself with her familiar tasks; perhaps then the

Above: American World War II propaganda, 1943.

feeling, glued like heavy plaster on her heart, would be gone. *Of all the stupid, despicable bullies*, she thought, pulling harder on Larry's hand. The child was still crying. Always before she had felt a tender pity for his defenseless little body, the frail arms, the narrow shoulders with sharp, winglike shoulder blades, the thin and unsure legs, but now her mouth tightened in resentment.

"Stop crying," she said sharply. "I'm ashamed of you!" She felt as if all three of them were tracking mud along the street. The child cried louder.

If there had been an issue involved, she thought, *if there had been something to fight for.... But what else could he possibly have done? Allow himself to be beaten? Attempt to educate the man? Call a policeman? "Officer, there's a man in the park who won't stop his child from throwing sand on mine...*. The whole thing was as silly as that, and not worth thinking about.

"Can't you keep him quiet, for Pete's sake?" Morton asked irritably.

"What do you suppose I've been trying to do?" she said.

Larry pulled back, dragging his feet.

"If you can't discipline this child, I will," Morton snapped, making a move toward the boy.

But her voice stopped him. She was shocked to hear it, thin and cold and penetrating with contempt. "Indeed?" she heard herself say. "You and who else?"

DIARY OF AN AMERICAN SLAVE

Frederick Douglass, 1845

M R. AUSTIN GORE. . . HAD SHOWN HIMSELF WORTHY OF THE HIGH STATION OF OVERSEER upon the home or Great House Farm.

Mr. Gore was proud, ambitious, and persevering. He was artful, cruel, and obdurate. He was just the man for such a place, and it was just the place for such a man. It afforded scope for the full exercise of all his powers, and he seemed to be perfectly at home in it. He was one of those who could torture the slightest look, word, or gesture, on the part of the slave, into impudence, and would treat it accordingly. There must be no answering back to him; no explanation was allowed a slave, showing himself to have been wrongfully accused. Mr. Gore acted fully up to the maxim laid down by slaveholders—"It is better that a dozen slaves should suffer under the lash, than that the overseer should be convicted, in the presence of the slaves, of having been at fault." No matter how innocent a slave might be—it availed him nothing, when accused by Mr. Gore of any misdemeanor. . . He was cruel enough to inflict the severest punishment, artful enough to descend to the lowest trickery, and obdurate enough to be insensible to

Left: Horace Pippin, *The Whipping.*

the voice of a reproving conscience. He was, of all the overseers, the most dreaded by the slaves. His presence was painful; his eye flashed confusion; and seldom was his sharp, shrill voice heard, without producing horror and trembling in their ranks. . . .

His savage barbarity was equalled only by the consummate coolness with which he committed the grossest and most savage deeds upon the slaves under his charge. Mr. Gore once undertook to whip one of Colonel Lloyd's slaves, by the name of Demby. He had given Demby but few stripes, when, to get rid of the scourging, he ran and plunged himself into a creek, and stood there at the depth of his shoulders, refusing to come out. Mr. Gore told him that he would give him three calls, and that, if he did not come out at the third call, he would shoot him. The first call was given. Demby made no response, but stood his ground. The second and third calls were given with the same result. Mr. Gore then, without consultation or deliberation with any one, not even giving Demby an additional call, raised his musket to his face, taking deadly aim at his standing victim, and in an instant poor Demby was no more. His mangled body sank out of sight, and blood and brains marked the water where he had stood.

A thrill of horror flashed through every soul upon the plantation, excepting Mr. Gore. He alone seemed cool and collected. He was asked by Colonel Lloyd and my old master, why he resorted to this extraordinary expedient. His reply was, (as well as I can remember,) that Demby had become unmanageable. He was setting a dangerous example to the other slaves,—one which, if suffered to pass without some such demonstration on his part, would finally lead to the total subversion of all rule and order upon the plantation. He argued that if one slave refused to be corrected, and escaped with his life, the other slaves would soon copy

The more that people are self-righteous and never live their shadow side, the more they project it and see others as the evildoers. The righteous live in a constant state of righteous indignation, hunting down their own shadow in the form of the other person.

—Marie von Franz

the example; the result of which would be, the freedom of the slaves, and the enslavement of the whites. Mr. Gore's defence was satisfactory. He was continued in his station as overseer upon the home plantation. His fame as an overseer went abroad. His horrid crime was not even submitted to judicial investigation. It was committed in the presence of slaves, and they of course could neither institute a suit, nor testify against him; and thus the guilty perpetrator of one of the bloodiest and most foul murders goes unwhipped of justice, and uncensured by the community in which he lives. Mr. Gore lived in St. Michael's, Talbot county, Maryland, when I left there; and if he is still alive, he very probably lives there now; and if so, he is now, as he was then, as highly esteemed and as much respected as though his guilty soul had not been stained with his brother's blood.

I speak advisedly when I say this,—that killing a slave, or any colored person, in Talbot county, Maryland, is not treated as a crime, either by the courts or the community. Mr. Thomas Lanman, of St. Michael's, killed two slaves, one of whom he killed with a hatchet, by knocking his brains out. He used to boast of the commission of the awful and bloody deed. I have heard him do so laughingly, saying, among other things, that he was the only benefactor of his country in the company, and that when others would do as much as he had done, we should be relieved of "the d—d niggers."

Y O U   F E L O N S   O N   T R I A L   I N   C O U R T S

Walt Whitman

YOU FELONS ON TRIAL IN COURTS,
You convicts in prison-cells, you sentenced assassins chained and hand-cuffed
with iron,
Who am I too that I am not on trial or in prison?
Me ruthless and devilish as any, that my wrists are not chained with iron, or
my ankles with iron?

You prostitutes flaunting over the trottoirs or obscene in your rooms,
Who am I that I should call you more obscene than myself?
O culpable! I acknowledge—I expose!
(O admirers, praise not me—compliment not me—you make me wince,
I see what you do not—I know what you do not.)

Inside these breast-bones I lie smutched and choked,
Beneath this face that appears so impassive hell's tides continually run,
Lusts and wickedness are acceptable to me,
I walk with delinquents with passionate love,
I feel I am of them—I belong to those convicts and prostitutes myself,
And henceforth I will not deny them—for how can I deny myself?

Right: Joseph Raymond McCarthy (1908-1957), politician and inquisitor, with his assistant Ray Cohn. McCarthy became famous for his investigations into supposedly communist subversion, and he persecuted some who were later seen as heroes. Both the McCarthy trials and the poem highlight the question of who should be on trial and who should not—who is innocent and who guilty—and of what?

THE WHALE

Herman Melville
Excerpt from *Moby Dick*

H IS THREE BOATS STOVE AROUND HIM, AND OARS AND MEN BOTH WHIRLING IN THE EDDIES; ONE CAPTAIN, SEIZING the line-knife from his broken prow, had dashed at the whale, as an Arkansas duellist at his foe, blindly seeking with a six inch blade to reach the fathom-deep life of the whale. That captain was Ahab. And then it was, that suddenly sweeping his sickle-shaped lower jaw beneath him, Moby Dick had reaped away Ahab's leg, as a mower a blade of grass in the field. No turbaned Turk, no hired Venetian or Malay, could have smote him with more seeming malice. Small reason was there to doubt, then, that ever since that almost fatal encounter, Ahab had cherished a wild vindictiveness against the whale, all the more fell for that in his frantic morbidness he at last came to identify with him, not only all his bodily woes, but all his intellectual and spiritual exasperations. The White Whale swam before him as the monomaniac incarnation of all those malicious agencies that some deep men feel eating in them, till they are left living on with half a heart and half a lung. That intangible malignity which has been from the beginning; to whose dominion even

Left: Ku Klux Klan initiation, circa 1925. The kneeling man is the initiate; a hooded Klan member stands over him with a chalice while other members stand in a circle around. Just as Ahab externalises his inner demons onto the whale, the KKK's demonizes those who do not conform to a single skin color and religious belief.

the modern Christians ascribe one-half of the worlds; which the ancient Ophites of the east reverenced in their statue devil; —Ahab did not fall down and worship it like them; but deliriously transferring its idea to the abhorred white whale, he pitted himself, all mutilated, against it. All that most maddens and torments; all that stirs up the lees of things; all truth with malice in it; all that cracks the sinews and cakes the brain; all the subtle demonisms of life and thought; all evil, to crazy Ahab, were visibly personified, and made practically assailable in Moby Dick. He piled upon the whale's white hump the sum of all the general rage and hate felt by his whole race from Adam down; and then, as if his chest had been a mortar, he burst his hot heart's shell upon it. . . .

Here, then, was this grey-headed, ungodly old man, chasing with curses Job's whale round the world, at the head of a crew, too, chiefly made up of mongrel renegades, and castaways, and cannibals—morally enfeebled also, by the incompetence of mere unaided virtue or right-mindedness in Starbuck, the invulnerable jollity of indifference and recklessness in Stubb, and the pervading mediocrity in Flask. Such a crew, so officered, seemed specially picked and packed by some infernal fatality to help him to his monomaniac revenge. How it was that they so aboundingly responded to the old man's ire—by what evil magic their souls were possessed, that at times his hate seemed almost theirs; the White Whale as much their insufferable foe as his; how all this came to be—what the White Whale was to them, or how to their unconscious understandings, also, in some dim, unsuspected way, he might have seemed the gliding great demon of the seas of life,—all this to explain, would be to dive deeper than Ishmael can go. The subterranean miner that works in us all, how can one tell whither leads his shaft by the ever shifting, muffled sound of his pick? Who does not feel the irresistible arm drag? What skiff in tow of a seventy-four can stand still? For one, I gave myself up to the abandonment of the time and the place; but while yet all a-rush to encounter the whale, could see naught in that brute but the deadliest ill.

Right: Jane Zich, *The Judges*.

As long as we maintain that all the evil is out there, our ship, like Ahab's is on the course of destruction. When we acknowledge that the capacity for evil lives within us as well, we can make peace with our shadow, and our ship can sail safely.

—Andrew Bard Schmookler

CHILDREN OF STRIKERS

Fred Chappell

THEY WERE WALKING, THE TWELVE-YEAR-OLD girl and the younger bleached-looking boy, by the edge of the black chemical river. A dreadful stink rose off the waters but they scarcely noticed it, scuffling along in the hard sawgrass among the stones. It was a dim day, rain-threatening, and the girl's dun face and dark eyes looked even darker than usual. The boy trailed some little distance behind her and would stop now and again and shade his eyes and look upstream and down. But there was no more reason for him to look about than there was for him to shade his eyes.

Occasionally the girl would bend down and look at something that caught her eye. A scrap of tin, a bit of drowned dirty cloth, jetsam thrown up from the river that poured through the paper factory above and then by the mill settlement behind them. This, "Fiberville," was a quadruple row of dingy little bungalows, and it was where the two of them lived. In the girl's dark face was something harsh and tired, as if she had foretold all her life and found it joyless.

Above: Phyllis Taplitz, *Triangle of Light.* **Right:** Migrant family during the Depression, Nipomo, California, March 1936. Both photograph and story illustrate the brutalizing effect of poverty.

Now she reached down and plucked something off a blackened wale of sand. She glanced at it briefly and thrust it into the pocket of her thin green sweater.

The boy had seen. He caught up with her and demanded to have a look.

"Look at what?" she asked.

"What you found, let me see it."

"It ain't nothing you'd care about."

"How do you know what I care? Let me have a look."

She turned to face him, gazed directly into his sallow annoying face, those milky blue eyes. "I ain't going to let you," she said.

He gave her a stare, then turned aside and spat. "Well, hell then, it ain't nothing."

"That's right." She walked on and he kept behind. But she knew he was gauging his chances, considering when to run and snatch it out of her pocket. When she heard his footsteps coming sneaky-fast, she wheeled and, without taking aim, delivered such a ringing slap that his eyes watered and his face flushed.

"God damn you," he said, but he didn't cry.

"I've told you to keep your hands away from me. I told you I wouldn't say it again."

"You ain't so much," he said. "I seen better." But his voice, though resentful, was not bitter.

They walked on a space and she began to relent. "It's a foot," she said.

"What you mean? What kind of foot?"

"It's a baby's foot."

"No!" He glared at her. "I ain't believing that."

"You can believe just whatever little thing you want to."

"I ain't believing you found no baby's foot. Let me see it."

"No."

"Well then, you ain't got nothing. . . . How big is it?"

"It's real tiny."

"Gaw," he said. It had seized his imagination. "Somebody probably kilt it."

"Might be."

"They must of kilt it and cut it up in little bits and throwed it in the river." He was wild with the thought of it. "It was some girl got knocked up and her boy friend made her do it."

She shrugged. "Ain't that awful to think about? A poor little baby. . . . Come on and show it to me. I got to see that baby foot."

"What'll you give me?"

They marched along, and he struck a mournful air. "Nothing," he said at last. "I ain't got nothing to give."

She stopped and looked at him, surveyed him head to toe with weary satisfaction. "No, I guess you ain't," she said. "You ain't got a thing."

"Well then, what you got? Nothing but a poor little dead baby's foot that I don't believe you've got anyhow."

Slowly she reached into her pocket and produced it, held it toward him in her open palm, and he leaned forward, breathless, peering. He shivered, almost imperceptibly. Then his face darkened and his eyes grew brighter and he slapped her hand. The foot jumped out of her hand and fell among the grasses.

"That ain't nothing. It's a doll, it's just a doll-baby's foot."

She could tell that he was disappointed but feeling smug too because, after all, he had caught her in the expectable lie. "I never told you it was real." She stopped and retrieved it. It lay pink and soiled in her soiled palm. Bulbous foot and ankle, little toes like beads of water. It looked too small and too separate from the rest of the world to be anything at all.

He took it from her. "I knowed it wasn't no real baby." He became thoughtful, turning it in his fingers. "Hey, look at this."

"I don't see nothing."

He held the tubular stub of it toward her. "Look how smooth it's cut off. It's been cut with a knife."

She touched it and the amputation was as smooth as the mouth of a soft drink bottle. "What's that got to do with anything?"

Inside everyone lurks a shadow. Behind the mask we wear for others, beneath the face we show ourselves, lives a hidden side of our personality. At night, while we lie helpless in our sleep, its image confronts us face to face.

—Fraser Boa

It had got darker now, drawing on toward the supper hour. Fiberville grew gloomier behind them, though most of the lights were on in the kitchens of the houses.

"Means that somebody went and cut it on purpose. . . ."

Another flushed fantasy overcame him. "Say, what if it was a Crazy Man? What if it was a man practicing up before he went and kilt a real baby?"

"It's just some little kid messing around," she said.

"Ain't no kid would have a knife like that." He ran his thumb over the edge of the cut. "Had to be a real *sharp* knife. Or an axe. Maybe it was a meat chopper!"

"Kid might get a knife anywhere."

He shook his head firmly. "No. Look how even it is and ain't hacked up. Kid would rag it up. A man went and done it, being real careful."

At last she nodded assent. Now at the same moment they turned and looked up the river bank into Fiberville, the squat darkening houses where the fathers and mothers and older sons now wore strained strange faces. The men didn't shave everyday now and the women cried sometimes. They had all turned into strangers, and among them at night in the houses were real strangers from far-off places saying hard wild sentences and often shouting and banging tabletops. In the overheated rooms both the light and the shadows loomed with an unguessable violence.

Right: John Marin, *Downtown, NY.* The painting evokes the sinister side of an urban environment.

Left: John Dillinger (1903-1934) attracted national attention for crimes in the Midwest over just 13 months in 1933 and 1934. He and his gang robbed banks and held up police stations to free captured members. J. Edgar Hoover of the Bureau of Investigation, now the FBI, nominated him Public Enemy No. 1, ensuring his place in American legend. The public was ambivalent about whether he was a hero or a villain given his daring in the hard times of the Depression. But how far are we our own worst enemy?
Right: Gangsters, circa 1935.

THE TELLTALE HEART

Edgar Allan Poe

TRUE!—NERVOUS—VERY, VERY DREADFULLY nervous I had been and am! but why will you say that I am mad? The disease had sharpened my senses—not destroyed—not dulled them. Above all was the sense of hearing acute. I heard all things in the heaven and in the earth. I heard many things in hell. How, then, am I mad? Hearken! and observe how healthily—how calmly I can tell you the whole story.

It is impossible to tell how first the idea entered my brain; but once conceived, it haunted me day and night. Object there was none. Passion there was none. I loved the old man. He had never wronged me. He had never given me insult. For his gold I had no desire. I think it was his eye! Yes, it was this! One of his eyes resembled that of a vulture—a pale blue eye, with a film over it. Whenever it fell upon me, my blood ran cold; and so by degrees—very gradually—I made up my mind to take the life of the old man, and thus rid myself of the eye forever.

Now this is the point. You fancy me mad. Madmen know nothing. But you should have seen *me*. You should have seen how wisely I proceeded—with what caution—with what foresight—with what dissimulation I went to work!

I was never kinder to the old man than during the whole week before I killed him. And every night, about midnight, I turned the latch of his door and opened it—oh, so gently! And then, when I had made an opening sufficient for my head, I put in a dark lantern, all closed, closed, so that no light shone out, and then I thrust in my head. Oh, you would have laughed to see how cunningly I thrust it in! I moved it slowly—very, very slowly, so that I might not disturb the old man's sleep. It took me an hour to place my whole head within the opening so far that I could see him as he lay upon his bed. Ha!—would a madman have been so wise as this? And then, when my head was well in the room, I undid the lantern cautiously—oh, so cautiously—cautiously (for the hinges creaked)—I undid it just so much that a single thin ray fell upon the vulture eye. And this I did for seven long nights—every night just at midnight—but I found the eye always closed; and so it was impossible to do the work; for it was not the old man who vexed me, but his Evil Eye. And every morning, when the day broke, I went boldly into the chamber, and spoke courageously to him, calling him by name in a hearty tone, and inquiring how he had passed the night. So you see he would have been a very profound old man, indeed, to suspect that every night, just at twelve, I looked in upon him while he slept.

Upon the eighth night I was more than usually cautious in opening the door. A watch's minute hand moves more quickly than did mine. Never before that night had I *felt* the extent of my own powers—of my sagacity. I could scarcely contain my feelings of triumph. To think that there I was, opening the door, little by little, and he not even to dream of my secret deeds or thoughts. I fairly chuckled at the idea; and perhaps he heard me; for he moved on the bed suddenly, as if startled. Now you may think that I drew back—but no. His room was as black as pitch with the thick darkness (for the shutters were close fastened, through fear of robbers), and so I knew that he could not see the opening of the door, and I kept pushing it on steadily, steadily.

I had my head in, and was about to open the lantern, when my thumb slipped upon the tin fastening, and the old man sprang up in bed, crying out: "Who's there?"

I kept quite still and said nothing. For a whole hour I did not move a muscle, and in the meantime I did not hear him lie down. He was still sitting up in the bed listening;—just as I have done, night after night, hearkening to the death watches in the wall.

Presently I heard a slight groan, and I knew it was the groan of mortal terror. It was not a groan of pain or grief—oh no!—it was the low stifled sound that arises from the bottom of the soul when overcharged with awe. I knew the sound well. Many a night, just at midnight, when all the world slept, it has welled up from my own bosom, deepening, with its dreadful echo, the terrors that distracted me. I say I knew it well. I knew what the old man felt, and pitied him, although I chuckled at heart. I knew that he had been lying awake ever since the first slight noise, when he had turned in the bed. His fears had been ever since growing upon him. He had been trying to fancy them causeless, but could not. He had been saying to himself: "It is nothing but the wind in the chimney—it is only a mouse crossing the floor," or "it is merely a cricket which has made a single chirp." Yes, he had been trying to comfort himself with these suppositions; but he had found all in vain. *All in vain*; because Death, in approaching him, had stalked with his black shadow before him, and enveloped the victim. And it was the mournful influence of the unperceived shadow that caused him to feel—although he neither saw nor heard—to *feel* the presence of my head within the room.

When I had waited a long time, very patiently, without hearing him lie down, I resolved to open a little— a very, very little crevice in the lantern. So I opened it—you cannot imagine how stealthily, stealthily—until, at length, a single dim ray, like the thread of the spider, shot from out the crevice and full upon the vulture eye.

It was open—wide, wide open—and I grew furious as I gazed upon it. I saw it with perfect distinctness—all a dull blue, with a hideous veil over it that chilled the very marrow in my bones; but I could see nothing else of the old man's face or person: for I had directed the ray, as if by instinct, precisely upon the damned spot.

And now—have I not told you that what you mistake for madness is but over-acuteness of the senses?—now, I say, there came to my ears a low, dull, quick sound, such as a watch makes when enveloped in cotton. I knew *that* sound well too. It was the beating of the old man's heart. It increased my fury, as the beating of a drum stimulates the soldier into courage.

But even yet I refrained and kept still. I scarcely breathed. I held the lantern motionless. I tried how steadily I could maintain the ray upon the eye. Meantime the hellish tattoo of the heart increased. It grew quicker and quicker, and louder and louder every instant. The old man's terror *must* have been extreme! It grew louder, I say, louder every moment!—do you mark me well? I have told you that I am nervous: so I am. And now at the dead hour of night, amid the dreadful silence of that old house, so strange a noise as this excited me to uncontrollable terror. Yet, for some minutes longer I refrained and stood still. But the beating grew louder,

louder! I thought the heart must burst. And now a new anxiety seized me—the sound would be heard by a neighbor! The old man's hour had come! With a loud yell, I threw open the lantern and leaped into the room. He shrieked once—once only. In an instant I dragged him to the floor, and pulled the heavy bed over him. I then smiled gaily, to find the deed so far done. But, for many minutes, the heart beat on with a muffled sound. This, however, did not vex me; it would not be heard through the wall. At length it ceased. The old man was dead. I removed the bed and examined the corpse. Yes, he was stone, stone dead. I placed my hand upon the heart and held it there many minutes. There was no pulsation. He was stone dead. His eye would trouble me no more.

If still you think me mad, you will think so no longer when I describe the wise precautions I took for the concealment of the body. The night waned, and I worked hastily, but in silence. First of all I dismembered the corpse. I cut off the head and the arms and the legs.

I then took up three planks from the flooring of the chamber, and deposited all between the scantlings. I then replaced the boards so cleverly, so cunningly, that no human eye—not even *his*—could have detected anything wrong. There was nothing to wash out—no stain of any kind—no blood-spot whatever. I had been too wary for that. A tub had caught all—ha! ha!

When I had made an end of these labors, it was four o'clock—still dark as midnight. As the bell sounded the hour, there came a knocking at the street door. I went down to open it with a light heart—for what had I now to fear? There entered three men, who introduced themselves, with perfect suavity, as officers of the police. A shriek had been heard by a neighbor during the night: suspicion of foul play had been aroused; information had been lodged at the police office, and they (the officers) had been deputed to search the premises.

Above: Paul LaMantia, *Day Thru Evening Dream.* There are places where the conscious and unconscious minds meet, such as the indefinable moment of time between dreaming and waking, madness or emotional extreme. In these meetings, the safe world we are accustomed to is recognizable but distorted. The artist here has captured such a moment on canvas; Edgar Allan Poe was a master of capturing such states in words.

I smiled—for *what* had I to fear? I bade the gentlemen welcome. The shriek, I said, was my own in a dream. The old man, I mentioned, was absent in the country. I took my visitors all over the house. I bade them search—search *well*. I led them, at length, to *his* chamber. I showed them his treasures, secure, undisturbed. In the enthusiasm of my confidence, I brought chairs into the room, and desired them *here* to rest from their fatigues, while I myself, in the wild audacity of my perfect triumph, placed my own seat upon the very spot beneath which reposed the corpse of the victim.

The officers were satisfied. My *manner* had convinced them. I was singularly at ease. They sat, and while I answered cheerily, they chatted familiar things. But, ere long, I felt myself getting pale and wished them gone. My head ached, and I fancied a ringing in my ears: but still they sat and still chatted. The ringing became more distinct:—it continued and became more distinct: I talked more freely to get rid of the feeling: but it continued and gained definiteness—until, at length, I found that the noise was *not* within my ears.

No doubt I now grew *very* pale,—but I talked more fluently, and with a heightened voice. Yet the sound increased—and what could I do? It was *a low, dull, quick sound—much such a sound as a watch makes when enveloped in cotton.* I gasped for breath—and yet the officers heard it not. I talked more quickly—more vehemently; but the noise steadily increased. Why *would* they not be gone? I paced the floor to and fro with heavy strides, as if excited to fury by the observation of the men—but the noise steadily increased. Oh, God; what *could* I do? I foamed—I raved—I swore! I swung the chair upon which I had been sitting, and grated it upon the boards, but the noise arose over all and continually increased. It grew louder—louder—*louder*! And still the men chatted pleasantly, and smiled. Was it possible they heard not? Almighty God!—no, no! They heard!—they suspected—they *knew*!—they were making a *mockery* of my horror!—this I thought, and this I think. But anything was better than this agony! Anything was more tolerable than this derision! I could bear those hypocritical smiles no longer! I felt that I must scream or die!—and now again!—hark! louder! louder! *louder*!

"Villains!" I shrieked, "dissemble no more! I admit the deed!—tear up the planks!—here, here!—it is the beating of his hideous heart!"

DIRECT MALE

Risa Mickenberg

A PRIVATE MESSAGE TO A SPECIAL friend.

Dear Annie Byrne:
This is a private invitation sent to you alone. I hope you'll accept my proposal. But even if you decide not to, I want to send you a gift. . . . **ABSOLUTELY FREE.**

Left: Andrew Lane, *Untitled.*

Yes. A 4 1/4" X 4 3/4" table-top calculator (battery included)—with a wide display screen and large keys will be delivered right to your door. You can't buy this fabulous calculator at any store in **New York**. But it can be yours . . . . without any obligation. . . simply by saying you'd like to have it!

Why I'm Writing To You

The list from which I selected your name indicates that you are a single, 34-year-old woman who earns $90,575, is concerned with fashion and health, has a cursory knowledge of politics, a bit of a Barney's addiction and a penchant for a certain discreet sex toy mail order catalog.

I like your profile.

I want you to marry me and as a FREE GIFT to you, Annie, you will receive the **marvelous table top calculator**.

How can I make such an incredible offer?

As Customer Service Representative for the Omni American Card, I see millions of interesting women in our database, but none whose spending habits and psychographic profile excite me the way yours do.
I'm confident that you will enjoy my sense of humor. My endearing mannerisms. My dog. **My full head of blonde hair.** You'll get it all when you marry me by **September 16, 1996.**
I'm sure you'll be delighted and intrigued by every little thing I do, Annie. Won't you accept this free calculator and be my wife?

Sincerely,
Richie Glickman
Customer Service Representative
Omni American Card

PS. This **FREE GIFT** offer expires after August 16,1996. I urge you to return it today.

* * *

OBITUARY
ANNIE BYRNE DIES, ALONE AND NEVER MARRIED, AT THE AGE OF 75.

Dear Miss Byrne:

A fictitious obituary? Perhaps.

But when it comes to finding a husband, the facts are grim:

> *There are over 250,000 single women in New York City
>> Murphy Brown ratings are at an all-time high.
>> This town is crawling with competition.

> *30% of the men deemed "eligible" by most surveys are actually prisoners. And fewer than 1/3 of those prisoners are serving sentences for white-collar crimes.

> *Pretty much everyone who's really fun is gay.

The fact is, there just aren't that many good men out there.

HOW MANY MORE NIGHTS CAN YOU SIT AT HOME ALONE WATCHING MARY TYLER MOORE ON NICK AT NIGHT AND EATING MOO SHU VEGETABLES?

You can't do it anymore, **Annie**, can you?

That's why I'm writing to you—to ask you to marry me. Please affix the YES sticker to the attached card and send the enclosed envelope with your answer today.

A legal marriage with me will protect you from the stigma of being a lonely old maid 24 hours a day, 7 days a week, anywhere in the world.

What is peace of mind like that worth these days?

Please marry me, Annie, before another gray hair appears on your head. **I've extended this unbelievable offer until October 15, 1996.** Mail your response today. Thank you.

> Sincerely Yours,
> *Richie Glickman*
> Customer Service Representative
> Omni American Card

* * *

Dear Ms Byrne:

Recently, I invited you to be my bride. My reason was clear. As a highly valued female cardmember, you <u>deserve</u> to join the select group of women who enter into matrimony.

Being married to me instantly identifies you as someone special. You'll enjoy a new degree of respect and attention from waitresses who formerly sneered, "Table for one?" at you or acted sympathetic which was even worse. You'll be instantly upgraded at hotels across the United States and around the world. You'll even be invited to more dinner parties.

The portfolio of benefits offered to you by marrying me will noticeably augment those you currently enjoy and will enhance the way you lead your life.

<u>Complimentary Companion Tickets to My Parents' Home in Minneapolis, Minnesota Every Thanksgiving</u>

Right: Federico Castellón, *The Dark Figure*. Who is the figure in the painting? We cannot tell, and yet she has a universal familiarity. What does the man in the story know about the woman he pursues?

With married life comes the joy of an extended family. "Mom" and "Dad" Glickman will welcome you every Thanksgiving with a home cooked meal, including yams, turkey and traditional stuffing, all with no salt added.

A Night Table for Your Side of The Bed

You will be entitled to a walnut night table to fill with photograph albums, bedtime reading and maybe even, God willing, baby books.

Safe Sex

You'll receive a signed certificate, suitable for framing from a qualified medical practitioner, ensuring that I am free from all sexually transmittable diseases—*a valuable thing to know in this day and age.*

It's O.K. I Was Up®
My Exclusive 24-Hour Listening Service

Whether you have a bad dream, or you're lying awake seething with rage over the way I leave my socks on the living room floor, or you're up at 4 a.m. convincing yourself you have cancer, you can wake me up and I'll listen. Really listen. You've earned this recognition and now I believe you should be wearing the ring that signifies your value: my wedding ring.

Sincerely,
Richie Glickman
Customer Service Representative
Omni American Card

      P.S. If you have already responded to my offer, please excuse this reminder letter. I just wanted to be sure you were aware of this very special offer.

* * *

Dear Miss Byrne:

Just what the hell were you doing spending $156 at **The Odeon** and $128 for tickets **Rent** last Thursday?

Never mind how I know.

I hope you haven't started dating. I've enclosed a brochure on the risks of rape, disease, attack and scam artistry. It's just plain stupid.

I want you. I want to marry you. I know we're perfect for each other.

It's not too late to respond.

Look. Meet me.

Let me help resolve whatever it is that's keeping you away. Simply bring this letter to my apartment at 190 Waverly Place #4B and redeem it for a FREE DINNER AT LA GRENOUILLE **worth well over $156**, you may rest assured.

Don't spend another night, or another cent, with some cheapskate loser you picked up God Knows Where.

Come over now and I'll never mention this little date of yours ever again, I swear.

Do we have a deal?

I look forward to seeing you.

Sincerely,
Richie Glickman
Customer Service Representative
Omni American Card

٨ ٨ ٨

DID I DO SOMETHING WRONG?

Dear Annie:

I haven't received your response.
I've sent you several notices, asking for your hand in marriage but I haven't received your answer.
Please take the time to fill out the response card and mail it back today. At this point, we'll be lucky If we can find a halfway decent place for the reception.

Cordially,
Richie Glickman
Customer Service Representative
Omni American Card

*   *   *

Dear Miss Byrne:

You've moved!

It's a busy time. New apartment, lots of unpacking to do, a bunch of light switches to figure out, a whole new life. You were probably too busy to send a simple change of address, right?

Don't apologize.
It's fine.

Chances are, when the craziness dies down and you're lying in that empty apartment, surrounded by empty boxes and wads of packing tape, you'll wish you bad someone—at least to help you reach those high shelves.

This is just a reminder that wherever you go, in every state and in 52 countries, whenever you need me, I am here. I can find you and be there in twelve hours.

Whether you need medical attention, a cash advance or you're finally ready to make a commitment that will provide you with the love, honor and respect you deserve, I'll always be here. 24 hours a day. A phone call away. Whenever you're ready. I will find you.

I look forward to hearing from you.

Sincerely,
Richie Glickman
Customer Service Representative
Omni American Card

MR.   AGREEABLE

Kirk Nesset

WHEN YOUR WIFE SAYS SHE'S LEAVING you do not object. You don't even let her know you're insulted—you've already foreseen the foreseeable, quaint as it sounds, and the business no longer shocks you. Politely, agreeably, you tell her to do as she pleases, watching the suitcases open and fill. You tell her to call when she can. Does she need any money? She says you shouldn't be so agreeable. You nod. You tend to agree.

In a world so rife with contention, why disagree? Some people you know—neighbors, in-laws, people you work with—home in on discord like heat-seeking missiles. They blast great holes in their lives, thriving on willful, blood-boiling chaos. This is not you—agreeable, peaceable you. Ready-made hardened opinion, you feel, goes quite against nature. It defies this earth we breathe and traverse on, which is fluid, they say, and constantly shifting, alive at the core.

Last year, before this business began, you saw your daughter committed. Foreseeable, foreseen. Your daughter, who wasn't ever quite "there" in the first place, thinks she's a cipher, that she is turning into the wind. Better that, of course, than a cave girl out of Ms. What's-her-name's novels, those books your daughter drank in to enter prehistory. When you visit you don't debate her absent identity. You agree to the terms. You offer your fatherly best as it were, fresh-shaved, patient, mildly heroic, compact and trim if a bit frayed at the edges; no need to let her know you're depressed. You bring her the weight of your affable nature, your humor, your unswerving desire to accept and agree, along with a snack of some kind, some candy, a bag of almonds or unsalted peanuts.

The visits increase once her mother is gone. Three, say or four times a week. The house has grown strange, to be truthful, and you like to get out. Your once-agreeable furnishings, the sofas and tables you decided to keep, have taken on auras, gray hazy outlines, which tend to unsettle. The bedroom exudes a disagreeable air. You hang around late at the office, rearranging your files; you visit your daughter. You sit in cafés on the weekends skimming the paper, thinking, deciding which movie to see. At night you awaken sitting upright in bed, discussing strange things with your curtains.

One Sunday, at an outdoor café, a man sits down at your table. He's thirty years younger than you, wide-shouldered, black-haired, bucktoothed. A fading tattoo on his hand. You come here a lot, he declares— he says he's seen you before. You do, you agree; he probably has. You're fond of the scones, you tell him. You glance at the crumbs on your plate.

Your agreeability, alas, makes you the ideal listener. People seem to sense this right off. You have a compassionate face, a kind face, you have

This American system of ours, call it Americanism, call it capitalism, call it what you will, gives each and every one of us a great opportunity if we only seize it with both hands and make the most of it.

—Al Capone

Right: Louis Guglielmi, *Terror in Brooklyn*. The women under the bell jar in a peculiar fragment of New York are a disturbing representation of entrapped grief and panic.

heard. Like a beacon, your face pulls people in, strangers out of accord with good fortune, survivors and talkers, victims of the shipwreck of living.

   The man has led a colorful life, as they say. He is funny, almost. You hear of his days as a kid in a much larger city, of all the hitchhiking he did, how for years he zigzagged the country, shacking up here, camping out there, he and a spotted castrated dog, a dog with one eye and one ear, a dog he called Lucky. You hear about his most recent romance.

   He entertains, you have to admit. His problems, so vivid and real, draw you away from your invented anxieties. You lean back and listen, agreeably nodding, sipping your tea. The ideal listener.

   So I blow into town, he says, fully into his story. I go up to the apartment and open the door, and guess what?

   You raise your eyebrows in question, unable to guess.

   My girlfriend's in there with Eddy, he says, this guy from downstairs.

   Delicacy forbids you to ask what were they doing, what did he see. You wipe your mouth with your napkin. You look at your watch. The story's growing less and less pleasant; you're afraid for the girl; you don't really like speaking with strangers. You take a few bills from your wallet and lay them down on the table.

   He asks if you're leaving, teeth extending out past his lip. You tell him your daughter is waiting. You've had a nice chat. He asks you which way you're headed. You tell him. He says he's going that way. You need to hear the rest of the story.

   Down the block by your car he says to hand over your billfold. The billfold, he says. You feel the nudge of the gun at your kidney.

   You are no crime-drama hero. You hand over the billfold, agreeing in full to his terms. He opens the wallet and scowls. You've never carried much cash on your person. Move up the street, he says—removing your bank card from its niche in the leather, tucking the gun in his pocket—we'll stop at the bank. You move up the sidewalk. Nervous, giddy, you ask what became of his girlfriend.

   I forgave her, he says, hands in his pockets. Then she skipped out.

   He slides your card in the slot at the bank. You stand side by side. He asks for your PIN, which you promptly reveal. He taps in the code.

   Silence. The street seems strangely deserted. You ask if he's found a new girlfriend.

   Shut up, he says. He stuffs the cash in his pocket. Story's over.

Half-joking, you ask if he'd mind if you kept the receipt.

Shut up, I said, he exclaims.

You begin to say that you're sorry—you don't quite shut up in time-and then the hand is out of the pocket, there's a blur of tattoo and you're down on your knees in the flowerbed, there among nasturtiums and lupine and poppies, reeling from the shock of the blow.

Don't be so shit-eating nice, he says, his shadow looming over like Neanderthal Man's. He says you remind him of Eddy, that two-faced adulterous creep. Lay flat on the ground now, he tells you. Don't move for five minutes. Down, if you ever want to get up.

You lie in the dirt on your belly, no hero, purely compliant. In a while you touch your scalp where he hit you, fearing there's blood; there isn't. You're lucky. The soil, barky and damp, clings to your fingers and hair. Your eyelashes brush against flowers—poppies, you think. Petals as vibrant as holiday pumpkins.

How long is five minutes?

People step up to get money. You hear them push in their cards and tap on the keyboard. You feel the individual discomfort, the dismay they endure to see such a sight, outlandish, right here out in the open, a man flung down on the ground in broad daylight, mashing the orange and blue flowers.

It seems you've been here forever. You've been here in dreams, you believe, in piecemeal visions—even this was foreseen in a way, if not quite clearly foreseeable. You should get up, you suppose, but you feel fine where you are. Sprawling, face in the black fragrant mulch, burrowing, digging in with your fingers, digging in like the wind. You press into the earth. The street grows quiet again. Ear to the ground, you hear plates trembling beneath you, weighty, incomprehensibly huge, aching with age and repeated collision, compelled by what is to agree and agree and agree.

SHADOWS OF LOVE

Mark Robert Waldman

The Bar

Y OU ARE SITTING IN A CHAIR BEFORE ME, BUT I DO NOT KNOW your name. I make love to your eyes, but they turn away, embarrassed and shy. I reach out to touch your lips with my finger, but your skin retreats, saying no. Not listening, I turn my gaze to your breasts, where the nipples lay hidden beneath your blouse. I ignore your discomfort and continue with my journey, down your belly, between your legs and around both thighs before descending to the floor. I have consumed you, devoured you, raped you. I feel satiated, fat. I light an imaginary cigarette and turn away, refusing to see the tear that has fallen on your cheek.

And I do not give a damn.

Chiron

A shadow sits upon my bed—her eyes, so full of tears. So many shadows on my wall, so many loves unseen. I am filled with shame and my eyes are covered with stones. I am but a paper shell, weak and calcium poor. We are shivering, waiting for a boat that never comes. We hold ourselves against the frightening black and try to kiss, but our lips have turned to sand. We see a distant light and cry out to the sea, but the ferryman cannot hear. We are the last—no more will come, no more will go from here. We sit upon an empty bed, we cannot live: two shadows unembraced.

Left: Edward Hopper, *Nighthawks.*

Left: Andrew Lane, *Untitled.* This photograph of
a man walking alone and bowed with age evokes
a sense of those who, having lost their life
partner, never manage to fill that emptiness. In
the story this poignancy is emphasized by
rejection and misunderstanding.
Right: Barry Peterson, *HF Gesture #10.*

THE MODEL

Bernard Malamud

EARLY ONE MORNING, EPHRAIM ELIHU RANG UP THE ART STUDENTS LEAGUE and asked the woman who answered the phone how he could locate an experienced female model he could paint nude. He told the woman that he wanted someone of about thirty. "Could you possibly help me?"

"I don't recognize your name," said the woman on the telephone. "Have you ever dealt with us before? Some of our students will work as models, but usually only for painters we know." Mr. Elihu said he hadn't. He wanted it understood he was an amateur painter who had once studied at the League.

"Do you have a studio?"

"It's a large living room with lots of light. I'm no youngster," he said, "but after many years I've begun painting again and I'd like to do some nude studies to get back my feeling for form. I'm not a professional painter, but I'm serious about painting. If you want any references as to my character, I can supply them."

He asked her what the going rate for models was, and the woman, after a pause, said, "Six dollars the hour."

Mr. Elihu said that was satisfactory to him. He wanted to talk longer, but she did not encourage him to. She wrote down his name and address and said she thought she could have someone for him the day after tomorrow. He thanked her for her consideration.

That was on Wednesday. The model appeared on Friday morning. She had telephoned the night before, and they had settled on a time for her to come. She rang his bell shortly after nine, and Mr. Elihu went at once to the door. He was a grayhaired man of seventy who lived in a brownstone house near Ninth Avenue, and he was excited by the prospect of painting this young woman.

The model was a plain-looking woman of twenty-seven or so, and the painter decided her best features were her eyes. She was wearing a blue raincoat, though it was a clear spring day. The old painter liked her but kept that to himself. She barely glanced at him as she walked firmly into the room.

"Good day," he said, and she answered, "Good day."

"It's like spring," said the old man. "The foliage is starting up again."

"Where do you want me to change?" asked the model.

Mr. Elihu asked her her name, and she responded, "Ms. Perry."

"You can change in the bathroom, I would say, Miss Perry, or if you like, my own room—down the hall—is empty, and you can change there also. It's warmer than the bathroom."

The model said it made no difference to her but she thought she would rather change in the bathroom.

"That is as you wish," said the elderly man.

"Is your wife around?" she then asked, glancing into the room.

"No, I happen to be a widower."

He said he had had a daughter once, but she had died in an accident.

The model said she was sorry.

"I'll change and be out in a few fast minutes."

"No hurry at all," said Mr. Elihu, glad he was about to paint her.

Ms. Perry entered the bathroom, undressed there, and returned quickly. She slipped off her terry-cloth robe. Her head and shoulders were slender and well formed. She asked the old man how he would like her to pose. He was standing by an enameltop kitchen table near a large window. On the tabletop he had squeezed out, and was mixing together, the contents of two small tubes of paint. There were three other tubes, which he did not touch. The model, taking a last drag of a cigarette, pressed it out against a coffee-can lid on the kitchen table.

"I hope you don't mind if I take a puff once in a while?"

"I don't mind, if you do it when we take a break."

"That's all I meant."

She was watching him as he slowly mixed his colors.

Mr. Elihu did not immediately look at her nude body but said he would like her to sit in the chair by the window. They were facing a back yard with an ailanthus tree whose leaves had just come out.

"How would you like me to sit, legs crossed or not crossed?"

"However you prefer that. Crossed or uncrossed doesn't make much of a difference to me. Whatever makes you feel comfortable."

The model seemed surprised at that, but she sat down in the yellow chair by the window and crossed one leg over the other. Her figure was good.

"Is this okay for you?"

Mr. Elihu nodded. "Fine," he said. "Very fine."

He dipped his brush into the paint he had mixed on the tabletop, and after glancing at the model's nude body, begin to paint. He would look at her, then look quickly away, as if he were afraid of affronting her . But his expression was objective. He painted apparently casually, from time to time gazing up at the model. He did not often look at her. She seemed not to be aware of him. Once she turned to observe the ailanthus tree, and he studied her momentarily to see what she might have seen in it.

Then she began to watch the painter with interest. She watched his eyes and she watched his hands. He wondered if he was doing something wrong. At the end of about an hour she rose impatiently from the yellow chair.

"Tired?" he asked.

"It isn't that," she said, "but I would like to know what in the name of Christ you think you are doing? I frankly don't think you know the first thing about painting."

She had astonished him. He quickly covered the canvas with a towel.

After a long moment, Mr.Elihu, breathing shallowly, wet his dry lips and said he was making no claims for himself as a painter. He said he had tried to make that absolutely clear to the woman he talked to at the art school when he called.

Then he said, "I might have made a mistake in asking you to come to this house today. I think I should have tested myself a while longer, just so I wouldn't be wasting anybody's time. I guess I am not ready to do what I would like to do."

"I don't care how long you have tested yourself," said Ms. Perry.

"I honestly don't think you have painted me at all. In fact, I felt you weren't interested in painting me. I think you're interested in letting your eyes go over my naked body for certain reasons of your own. I don't know what your personal needs are, but I'm damn well sure that most of them have nothing to do with painting."

Above: *Barry Peterson, P Gesture #2.*

"I guess I have made a mistake."

"I guess you have," said the model. She had her robe on now, the belt pulled tight.

"I'm a painter," she said, "and I model because I am broke, but I know a fake when I see one."

"I wouldn't feel so bad," said Mr. Elihu, "if I hadn't gone out of my way to explain the situation to that lady at the Art Students League.

"I'm sorry this happened," Mr. Elihu said hoarsely. "I should have thought it through more than I did. I'm seventy years of age. I have always loved women and felt a sad loss that I have no particular women friends at this time of my life. That's one of the reasons I wanted to paint again, though I make no claims that I was ever greatly talented. Also, I guess I didn't realize how much about painting I have forgotten. Not only about that, but also about the female body. I didn't realize I would be so moved by yours, and, on reflection, about the way my life has gone. I hoped painting again would refresh my feeling for life. I regret that I have inconvenienced and disturbed you."

"I'll be paid for my inconvenience," Ms. Perry said, "but what you can't pay me for is the insult of coming here and submitting myself to your eyes crawling on my body."

"I didn't mean it as an insult."

"That's what it feels like to me."

She then asked Mr. Elihu to disrobe.

"I?" he said, surprised. "What for?"

"I want to sketch you. Take your pants and shirt off."

He said he had barely got rid of his winter underwear, but she did not smile.

Mr. Elihu disrobed, ashamed of how he must look to her.

With quick strokes she sketched his form. He was not a badlooking man, but felt bad. When she had the sketch, she dipped his brush into a blob of black pigment she had squeezed out of a tube and smeared his features, leaving a black mess.

He watched her hating him, but said nothing.

Ms. Perry tossed the brush into a wastebasket and returned to the bathroom for her clothing.

The old man wrote out a check for her for the sum they had agreed on. He was ashamed to sign his name, but he signed it and handed it to her. Ms. Perry slipped the check into her large purse and left.

He thought that in her way she was not a bad-looking woman, though she lacked grace. The old man then asked himself, "Is there nothing more to my life than it is now? Is this all that is left to me?"

The answer seemed to be yes, and he wept at how old he had so quickly become.

Afterward he removed the towel over his canvas and tried to fill in her face, but he had already forgotten it.

THE   DEAD   BOY   AT
YOUR   WINDOW

Bruce Holland Rogers

I N A DISTANT COUNTRY WHERE THE towns had improbable names, a woman looked upon the unmoving form of her newborn baby and refused to see what the midwife saw. This was her son. She had brought him forth in agony, and now he must suck. She pressed his lips to her breast.

"But he is dead!" said the midwife.

"No," his mother lied. "I felt him suck just now." Her he was as milk to the baby, who really was dead but who now opened his dead eyes and began to kick his dead legs. "There, do you see?" And she made the midwife call the father in to know his son.

The dead boy never did suck at his mother's breast. He sipped no water, never took food of any kind, so of course he never grew. But his father, who was

Above: From the Burning Man Festival 2001, photograph by Tony Pletts. Detail of a tree built from bones.
Right: Jane Zich, *The Navigator.*

handy with all things mechanical, built a rack for stretching him so that, year by year, he could be as tall as the other children.

When he had seen six winters, his parents sent him to school. Though he was as tall as the other students, the dead boy was strange to look upon. His bald head was almost the right size, but the rest of him was thin as a piece of leather and dry as a stick. He tried to make up for his ugliness with diligence, and every night he was up late practicing his letters and numbers.

His voice was like the rasping of dry leaves. Because it was so hard to hear him, the teacher made all the other students hold their breaths when he gave an answer. She called on him often, and he was always right.

Naturally, the other children despised him. The bullies sometimes waited for him after school, but beating him, even with sticks, did him no harm. He wouldn't even cry out.

Above: Jane Zich, detail of *Lost Constellation.*

One windy day, the bullies stole a ball of twine from their teacher's desk, and after school, they held the dead boy on the ground with his arms out so that he took the shape of a cross. They ran a stick in through his left shirt sleeve and out through the right. They stretched his shirt tails down to his ankles, tied everything in place, fastened the ball of twine to a button-hole, and launched him. To their delight, the dead boy made an excellent kite. It only added to their pleasure to see that owing to the weight of his head, he flew upside down.

When they were bored with watching the dead boy fly, they let go of the string. The dead boy did not drift back to earth, as any ordinary kite would do. He glided. He could steer a little, though he was mostly at the mercy of the winds. And he could not come down. Indeed, the wind blew him higher and higher.

The sun set, and still the dead boy rode the wind. The moon rose and by its glow he saw the fields and forests drifting by. He saw mountain ranges pass beneath him, and oceans and continents. At last the winds gentled, then ceased, and he glided down to the ground in a strange country. The ground was bare. The moon and stars had vanished from the sky. The air seemed gray and shrouded. The dead boy leaned to one side and shook himself until the stick fell from his shirt. He wound up the twine that had trailed behind him and waited for the sun to rise. Hour after long hour, there was only the same grayness. So he began to wander.

He encountered a man who looked much like himself, a bald head atop leathery limbs. "Where am I?" the dead boy asked.

The man looked at the grayness all around. "Where?" the man said. His voice, like the dead boy's, sounded like the whisper of dead leaves stirring.

A woman emerged from the grayness. Her head was bald, too, and her body dried out. "This!" she rasped, touching the dead boy's shirt. "I remember this!" She tugged on the dead boys sleeve. "I had a thing like this!"

"Clothes?" said the dead boy.

"Clothes!" the woman cried. "That's what it is called!"

More shriveled people came out of the grayness. They crowded close to see the strange dead boy who wore clothes. Now the dead boy knew where he was. "This is the land of the dead."

"Why do you have clothes?" asked the dead woman. "We came here with nothing! Why do you have clothes?"

"I have always been dead," said the dead boy, "but I spent six years among the living."

"Six years!" said one of the dead. "And you have only just now come to us?"

"Did you know my wife?" asked a dead man. "Is she still among the living?"

"Give me news of my son!"

"What about my sister?"

The dead people crowded closer.

The dead boy said, "What is your sister's name?" But the dead could not remember the names of their loved ones. They did not even remember their own names. Likewise, the names of the places where they had lived, the numbers given to their years, the manners or fashions of their times, all of these they had forgotten.

"Well," said the dead boy, "in the town where I was born, there was a widow. Maybe she was your wife. I knew a boy whose mother had died, and an old woman who might have been your sister."

"Are you going back?"

"Of course not," said another dead person. "No one ever goes back."

"I think I might," the dead boy said. He explained about his flying. "When next the wind blows. . . ."

"The wind never blows here," said a man so newly dead that he remembered wind.

"Then you could run with my string."

"Would that work?"

"Take a message to my husband!" said a dead woman.

"Tell my wife that I miss her!" said a dead man.

"Let my sister know I haven't forgotten her!"

"Say to my lover that I love him still!"

They gave him their messages, not knowing whether or not their loved ones were themselves long dead. indeed, dead lovers might well he standing next to one another in the land of the dead, giving messages for each other to the dead boy. Still, he memorized them all. Then the dead put the stick back inside his shirt sleeves, tied everything in place, and unwound his string. Running as fast as their leathery legs could manage, they pulled the dead boy back into the sky, let go of the string, and watched with their dead eyes as he glided away.

He glided a long time over the gray stillness of death until at last a puff of wind blew him higher, until a breath of wind took him higher still, until a gust of wind carried him up above the grayness to where he could see the moon and the stars. Below he saw moonlight reflected in the ocean. In the distance rose mountain peaks. The dead boy came to earth in a little village. He knew no one here, but he went to the first house he came to and rapped on the bedroom shutters. To the woman who answered, he said, "A message from the land of the dead," and gave her one of the messages. The woman wept, and gave him a message in return.

House by house, he delivered the messages. House by house, he collected messages for the dead. In the morning, he found some boys to fly him, to give him back to the wind's mercy so he could carry these new messages back to the land of the dead.

So it has been ever since. On any night, head full of messages, he may rap upon any window to remind someone—to remind you, perhaps—of love that outlives memory, of love that needs no names.

Left: Ivan Albright, *Poor Room—There is No Time, No End, No Today, No Yesterday, No Tomorrow, Only the Forever, and Forever and Forever Without End (The Window).*

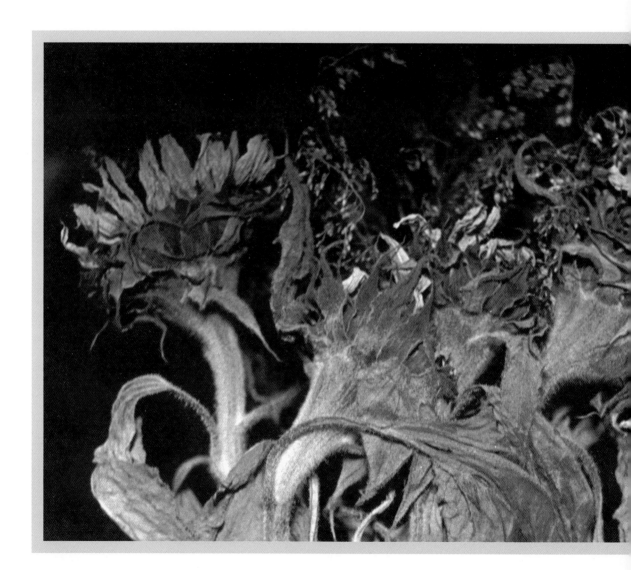

SURVIVORS

Kim Addonizio

He and his lover were down to their last few T cells and arguing over who was going to die first. He wanted to be the first because he did not want to have to take care of his lover's parrot or deal with his lover's family, which would descend on their flat after the funeral, especially the father, who had been an Army major and had tried to beat his son's sexual orientation out of him with a belt on several occasions during adolescence; the mother, at least, would be kind but sorrowful, and secretly blame him, the survivor—he knew this from her letters, which his lover had read to him each week for the past seven years. He knew, too, that they all—mother, two older brothers—would disapprove of their flat, of the portrait of the two of them holding hands that a friend had painted and which hung over the bed, the Gay Freedom Day poster in the bathroom, all the absurd little knickknacks like the small plastic wind-up penis that hopped around on two feet; maybe, after his lover died, he would put some things away, maybe he would even take the parrot out of its cage and open the window so it could join the wild ones he'd heard of that nested in the palm trees on Dolores Street, a whole flock of bright tropical birds apparently thriving in spite of the chilly Bay Area weather—he would let it go, fly off, and he would be completely alone then; dear God, he thought, let me die first, don't let me survive him.

Left: Andrew Lane, *Untitled*. Sunflowers are usually a symbol of life, but here they are photographed dead. Any writing about young men dying can only leave a similar sense of bewilderment, the same sense of a disjunction in the natural order of things.

THE SIGNING

Stephen Dixon

M Y WIFE DIES. NOW I'M ALONE. I KISS HER HANDS AND LEAVE THE HOSPITAL ROOM. A NURSE RUNS AFTER ME AS I WALK down the hall.

"Are you going to make arrangements now for the deceased?" he says.

"No."

"Then what do you want us to do with the body?"

"Burn it."

"That's not our job."

"Give it to science."

"You'll have to sign the proper legal papers."

"Give me them."

"They take a while to draw up. Why don't you wait in the guest lounge?"

"I haven't time."

"And her toilet things and radio and clothes."

"I have to go." I ring for the elevator.

"You can't do that."

"I am."

The elevator comes.

"Doctor, doctor," he yells to a doctor going through some files at the nurses' station. She stands up. "What is it nurse?" she says. The elevator door closes. It opens on several floors before it reaches the lobby. I head for the outside. There's a security guard sitting beside the revolving door. He looks like a regular city

Right: The funeral of president John F. Kennedy, Washington DC, November 25, 1963. The assassination of the President brought the devastating shock of bereavement not only to America, but it also reverberated around the world. After the Kennedy assassination, grief was public and great sympathy went out to the Kennedy family. In the story, no such dignity is afforded to the main character as his emotional needs remain at odds with those around him.

policeman other than for his hair, which hangs down past his shoulders, and he also has a beard. Most city policemen don't; maybe all. He gets a call on his portable two-way set as I step into one of the quarters of the revolving door. "Laslo," he says into it. I'm outside. "Hey you," he says. I turn around. He's nodding and pointing to me and waves for me to come back. I cross the avenue to get to the bus stop. He comes outside and slips the two-way into his back pocket and walks up to me as I wait for the bus.

"They want you back upstairs to sign some papers," he says.

"Too late. She's dead. I'm alone. I kissed her hands. You can have the body. I just want to be far away from here and as soon as I can."

"They asked me to bring you back."

"You can't. This is a public street. You need a city policeman to take me back, and even then I don't think he or she would be in their rights."

"I'm going to get one."

The bus comes. Its door opens. I have the required exact fare. I step up and put my change in the coin box.

"Don't take this man," the guard says to the bus driver. "They want him back at the hospital there. Something about his wife who was or is a patient, though I don't know the actual reason they want him for."

"I've done nothing," I tell the driver and take a seat in the rear of the bus. A woman sitting in front of me says, "What's holding him up? This isn't a red light."

"Listen," the driver says to the guard, "if you have no specific charge or warrant against this guy, I think I better go."

"Will you please get this bus rolling again?" a passenger says.

"Yes," I say, disguising my voice so they won't think it's me but some other passenger, "I've an important appointment and your slowpokey driving and intermittent dawdling has already made me ten minutes late."

The driver shrugs at the guard. "In or out, friend, but unless you can come up with some official authority to stop this bus, I got to finish my run."

The guard steps into the bus, pays his fare, and sits beside me as the bus pulls out.

"I'll have to stick with you and check in if you don't mind," he says to me. He pushes a button in his two-way set and says "Laslo here."

"Laslo," a voice says. "Where the hell are you?"

"On a bus."

"What are you doing there? You're not through yet."

"I'm with the man you told me to grab at the door. Well, he got past the door. I tried to stop him outside, but he said I needed a city patrolman for that because it was a public street."

"You could've gotten him on the sidewalk in front."

"This was at the bus stop across the street."

"Then he's right. We don't want a suit."

"That's what I thought. So I tried to convince him to come back. He wouldn't. He said he'd kissed some woman's hands and we can have the body. I don't know what that means but want to get it all in before I get too far away from you and lose radio contact. He got on this bus. The driver was sympathetic to my argument about the bus not leaving, but said it would be illegal his helping to restrain the man and that he also had to complete his run. So I got on the bus and am now sitting beside the man and will get of at the next stop if that's what you want me to do. I just didn't know what was the correct way to carry out my orders in this situation, so I thought I'd stick with him till I found out from you."

"You did the right thing. Let me speak to him now."

Laslo holds the two-way in front of my mouth. "Hello," I say.

"The papers to donate your wife's body to the hospital for research and possible transplants are ready now, sir, so could you return with Officer Laslo?"

"No."

"If you think it'll be too trying an emotional experience to return here, could we meet someplace else where you could sign?"

"Do what you want with her body. There's nothing I ever want to have to do with her again. I'll never speak her name. Never go back to our apartment. Our car I'm going to let rot in the street till it's towed away. This wristwatch. She bought it for me and wore it a few times herself." I throw it out the window.

"Why didn't you just pass it on back here?" the man behind me says.

"These clothes. She bought some of them, mended them all." I take off my jacket, tie, shirt and pants and toss them out the window.

"Lookit," Laslo says, "I'm just a hospital security guard with a pair of handcuffs I'm not going to use on

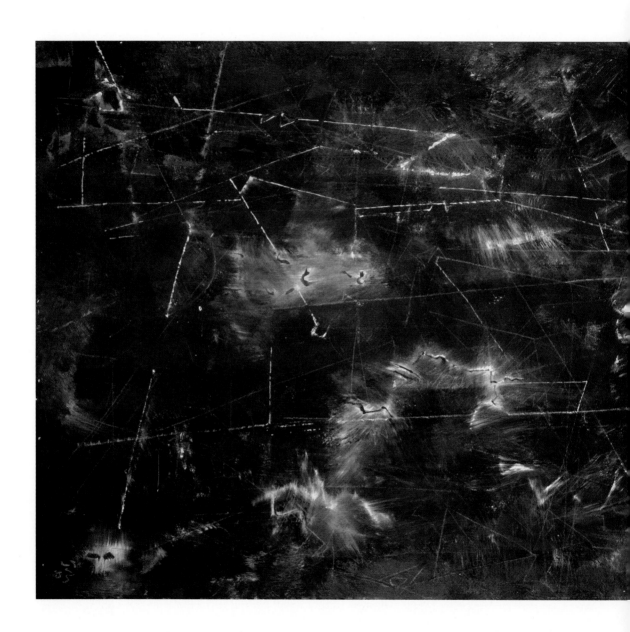

you because we're in a public bus and all you've just gone through, but please calm down."

"This underwear I bought myself yesterday," I say to him. "I needed a new pair. She never touched or saw them, so I don't mind still wearing them. The shoes go, though. She even put on these heels with a shoe-repair kit she bought at the five-and-dime." I take of my shoes and drop them out the window.

The bus has stopped. All the other passengers have left except Laslo. The driver is on the street looking for what I'm sure is a patrolman or police car.

I look at my socks. "I'm not sure about the socks."

"Leave them on," Laslo says. "They look good, and I like brown."

"But did she buy them? I think they were a gift from her two birthdays ago when she gave me a cane picnic basket with a dozen-and-a-half pairs of different-colored socks inside. Yes, this is one of them," and I take them off and throw them out the window. "That's why I tried and still have to get out of this city fast as 1 can."

"You hear that?" Laslo says into the two-way radio, and the man on the other end says, "I still don't understand."

"You see," I say into it, "we spent too many years here together, my beloved and I—all our adult lives. These streets. That bridge. Those buildings." I spit out the window. "Perhaps even this bus. We took so many rides up and down this line." 1 try to uproot the seat in front of me but it won't budge. Laslo claps the cuffs on my wrists. "This life," I say and I smash my head through the window.

An ambulance comes and takes me back to the same hospital. I'm brought to Emergency and put on a cot in the same examining room she was taken to this last time before they moved her to a semiprivate room. A hospital official comes in while the doctors and nurses are tweezing the remaining glass splinters out of my head and stitching me up. "If you're still interested in donating your wife's body," he says, "then we'd like to get the matter out of the way while some of her organs can still be reused by several of the patients upstairs."

I say, "No, I don't want anyone walking around with my wife's parts where I can bump into him and maybe recognize them any day of the year," but he takes my writing hand and guides it till I've signed.

Left: Mark Tobey, *Above the Earth.* Grief distances you from normal day-to-day events.

PLEASE   REMAIN   CALM

A. M. Homes

I WISH I WERE DEAD. I HAVE TRIED TO KEEP it a secret, but it leaks out: "I wish I were dead," I blurted to the woman who is now my wife, the first morning we woke up together, the sheets still hot, stinking of sex.

"Should I take it personally?" she asked, covering herself.

"No," I said and began to cry.

"It's not so easy to die," she says.

And she should know, she's a woman whose milieu is disaster—a specialist in emergency medicine. All day she is at work, putting the pieces back together and then she comes home to me. She tells me about the man run over by a train, how they carried in each of his legs in separate canvas bags. She tells me about the little boy doused in oil and deep-fried.

"Hi honey, I'm home," she says.

I hold my breath.

"I know you're here, your briefcase is in the front hall. Where are you?"

I wait to answer.

"Honey?"

I am sitting at the kitchen table.

Above: Georgia O'Keeffe, *Dark Mesa with Pink Sky.*   **Right:** John Henshaw, *Driver-NYC.* In a drawing evocative of Munch's The Scream, a driver reaches crisis.

"Today's the day," I tell her.

"What's different today?" she asks.

"Nothing. Nothing is different about today—that's the point. I feel the same today as I did yesterday and the day before. It's insufferable. Today," I repeat.

"Not today," she says.

"Now's the time," I say.

"Not the time."

"The moment has come."

"The moment has passed."

Every day I wish I didn't have to live a minute more; I wish I were someplace else, someplace new, someplace that never existed before. Death is a place without history; it's not like people have been there and then come back to tell you what a great time they had, that they highly recommend it, the food is wonderful and there's an incredible hotel right on the water.

"You think death is like Bali," my wife says.

We have been married for almost two years; she doesn't believe me anymore. It is as though I've cried wolf, screamed wolf, been a wolf, too many times.

"Did you stop at the store?"

I nod. I am in charge of the perishables, the things that must be consumed immediately. Every day on my way home, I shop. Before I was married I would buy only one of each thing, a bottle of beer, a can of soup, a single roll of toilet paper—that sounds fine on a Monday when you think there will be no Tuesday, but what about late on Friday night when the corner store is closed?

My wife buys in bulk, she is forever stocking up; she is prepared in perpetuity.

"Did you remember milk?"

"I bought a quart."

"Not a half gallon?"

"You're lucky it's not a pint."

We are vigilant people, equally determined. The ongoing potential for things to go wrong is our bond— she likes to repair and I to wallow, to roll obsessively in the possibilities like some perverted pig. It is a control issue, maintaining control for as long as possible. Our closets are packed with emergency supplies: bottles of water, a backup generator, air purifiers, fire extinguishers, freeze-dried food, medical supplies, a stack of two hundred dollar bills, his and hers cans of mace, we are ready and waiting.

She opens a beer and flips through a catalog for emergency management specialists. This is how she relaxes-"What about gas masks? What if something happens, what if there's an event?" She checks off the box for gas masks and then goes for a couple of smoke hoods. "They're good for traveling. All the FAA guys carry their own, it's a little known fact, smoke inhalation is a major cause of death on airplanes."

"I'm not surprised." I open a beer, take a breath. "I can't stand it anymore."

"You're stronger than you think."

I have spent nights laid low near the exhaust pipe of a car, have slept with a plastic bag over my head and silver duct tape around my neck. I have rifled through the kitchen drawers at three a.m. thinking I will have at myself with a carving knife. There have been mornings when I've taken my straight razor to my throat and carved. Once fresh from the shower, I divided myself in half, a clean incision from sternum to pubis. In the bathroom mirror, I watched what was leaking out of me, escaping me, with peculiar pleasure not unlike the perverse pleasantry of taking a good shit. I arrived at the office dotted with the seeping red of my efforts. "Looks like you got a little on you," my secretary said, donating her seltzer to blot the spot. "You're always having these shaving accidents. Maybe you're cutting it too close."

All the above is only a warm-up, a temporizing measure, a palliative remedy, I want something more, the big bang. If I had a gun I would use it, again and again, a million times a day I would shoot myself.

"What do you want to do about dinner?"

"Nothing. I never want to eat again."

"Not even steak?" my wife asks. "I was thinking I'd make us a nice

The ego. . .is in conflict with the shadow, in what Dr. Jung once called "the battle for deliverance." In the struggle of primitive man to achieve consciousness, the conflict is expressed the contest between the archetypal hero and the cosmic powers of evil, personified by dragons and other monsters. . . . For most people the dark or negative side of the personality remains unconscious. The hero, on the contrary, must realize that the shadow exists and that he can draw strength from it. He must come to terms with the destructive powers if he is to become sufficiently terrible to overcome the dragon. I.e., before the ego can triumph, it must master and assimilate the shadow.

——Joseph Henderson

thick steak. Yesterday you said, 'How come we never have steak anymore?' I took one out of the deep freeze this morning."

"Don't try and talk me out of it."

"Fine, but I'm having steak. Let me know if you change your mind."

There is a coldness to her, a chill I find terrifying an absence of emotion that puts a space between us, a permanent and unbridgeable gap—I am entirely emotion, she is entirely reason.

I will not change my mind. This isn't something new, something that started late in life. I've been this way since I was a child. It is the most awful addiction-the opposite of being a vampire and living off the blood of others, "eripmav"—sucked backward through life, the life cycle run in reverse, beginning in death and ending in. . . .

Short of blowing my brains out, there is no way I can demonstrate the intensity, the extremity of my feeling. Click. Boom. Splat. The pain is searing, excruciating; the roots of my brain are hot with it.

"You can't imagine the pain I'm in."

"Take some Tylenol."

"Do you want me to make a salad?"

I have been married before, did I mention that? It ended badly—I ran into my ex-wife last week on the street and the color drained from both our faces—we're still weak from memory. "Are you all right?" I wondered.

"I'm better," she said. "Much better. Alone." She quickly walked away.

There is an enormous amount of tension in being with someone who is dying every day. It's a perpetual hospice; the grief is too extreme. That's my specialty, pushing the limits, constantly testing people. No one can pass—that is the point. In the end, they crack, they leave and I blame them.

I'm chopping lettuce.

"Caesar," my wife says and I look up. She hands me a tin of anchovies. "Use the romaine."

"How was work?" There is relief in other people's tragedies.

"Interesting" she says, pulling the meat out of the broiler. She slices open the steak, blood runs out.

"How does that look?"

"Perfect." I smile, grating the parmesan.

"A guy came in this afternoon, high on something. He'd tried to take his face off, literally—took a knife and peeled it."

"How did you put him back together?"

"A thousand stitches and surgical glue. Another man lost his right hand. Fortunately, he's a lefty."

We sit at the kitchen table talking about severed limbs, thin threads of ligaments, the delicate weave of nerves—reattachment, the hope of regaining full function. Miracles.

"I love you," she says, leaning over, kissing my forehead.

"How can you say that?"

"Because I do?"

"You don't love me enough."

"Nothing is enough," she says. And it is true, excruciatingly true.

I want to tell her I am having an affair, I want to make her leave, I want to prove that she doesn't love me enough. I want to have it over with.

"I'm having an affair," I tell her.

"No, you're not."

"Yes, I am. I'm fucking Sally Baumgarten."

She laughs. "And I'm giving blowjobs to Tom."

"My friend Tom?"

"You bet."

She could be, she very well could be. I pour Cascade into the dishwasher and push the button—Heavy Soil.

"I'm leaving" I tell her.

"Where are you going?"

"I don't know."

"When will you be back?"

"Never. I'm not coming back."

Then you're not leaving," she says.

"I hate you."

I married her before I loved her. For our honeymoon, we went to California. She was thinking

Disneyland, Carmel, Big Sur, a driving trip up the coast—fun. I was hoping for an earthquake, brush fire, mudslide—disaster.

In the hotel room in Los Angeles I panicked. A wall of glass, a broad expanse of windows looking out over the city—it was a surprisingly clear night. The lights in the hills twinkled, beckoned. Without warning I ran toward the glass, hurling myself forward.

She took me down, tackling me. She sat on top, pinning me, her one hundred nineteen pounds on my one fifty-six—she's stronger than you think.

"If you do that again I won't forgive you."

The intimacy, the unbearable intimacy is what's most mortifying—when they know the habits of your bowels, your cheapnesses, your horribleness, when they know things about you that no one should know, things you don't even know about yourself.

She knows these things and doesn't say it's too much, too weird, too fucked up. "It's my training," she says. "My shift doesn't end just because something bad happens."

It is about love. It is about getting enough, having enough, drowning in it, and now it is too late. I am permanently malnourished—there isn't enough love in the world.

There is a danger in this, in writing this, in saying this. I am putting myself on the line. If I am found floating face down, there will be theories, lingering questions. Did he mean it? Was it an accident—is there any such thing as an accident, is fate that forgiving? Was this letter a warning, a true story? Everything is suspect. (Unless otherwise instructed—if something happens, give me the benefit of the doubt.)

"What would it be like if you gave it up?" she asked.

I am incredulous.

"If you abandoned the idea? Aren't you bored by it all after all these years; why not just give it up?"

"Wanting to be dead is as natural to me as breathing."

What would I be without it? I don't know that I could handle it. Like being sprung from a lifetime jail, like Jack Henry Abbot, I might wheel around and stab someone with a dinner knife.

Right: John Rogers Cox, *Gray & Gold.*

And what if I truly gave it up, if I said, Yes it is a beautiful day, yes I am incredibly lucky—one of the luckiest men in the world. What if I admitted it, You are my best friend, my favorite fuck, my cure. What if I say I love you and she says, It's over. What if that's part of the game, the dance? I will have missed my moment, I will be shit out of luck—stuck here forever.

"Why do you put up with it?"

"Because this is not you," she says. "It's part of you, but it's not you. Are you still going to kill yourself?

"Yes," I say. Yes I am, to prove I am independent, to prove I still can. "I hate you," I tell her. "I hate you so much."

"I know," she says.

My wife is not without complications of her own. She keeps a baseball bat under her side of the bed. I discovered it by accident—one day it rolled out from under. Louisville Slugger. I rolled it back into place and have never let on that I know it's there. Sometimes she wakes up in the middle of the night, sits straight up and screams, "Who is out there? Who is in the waiting room?" She stops for a second and starts again, annoyed, "I don't have all day. Next. Bring the next one in." There are nights I watch her sleep, her face a naive dissolve, tension erased, her delicate blond lashes, her lips, soft like a child and I want to punch her. I want to bash her face in. I wonder what she would do then.

"A thought is only a thought," she says when I wake her, when I tell her what I was thinking.

Then she tells me her dreams. "I was a man and I was having sex with another man and you were there, you were wearing a white skirt, and then someone came in but he didn't have any arms and I kept wondering how did he open the door?"

"Let's go back to sleep for a little while."

I am getting closer. The situation is untenable, something has to happen. I have lived this way for a long time; there is a cumulative effect, a worsening. I am embarrassed that I have let it go on for so long.

I know how I will do it. I will hang myself. Right here at home. I have known it since we bought the house. When the real estate agent went on and on about the location, the yard, the school district, I was thinking about the interior—the exposed rafters, the beams. The dead man's walk to the top of the stairs.

We are cleaning up. I wipe the table with a sponge.

"What's in the bag?" she says, pointing to something on the counter.

"Rope." I stopped on the way home. I ran the errand.

"Let's go to the movies," she says, tying up the trash. She hands me the bag. "Take it outside," she says, sending me into the night.

The yard is flooded with light, extra lights, like search lights, lights so bright that when raccoons cross to get to the trash, they hold their paws up over their eyes, shielding them.

I feel her watching me from the kitchen window.

We go to see *The Armageddon Complex*, a disaster film with a tidal wave, a tornado, a fire, a global-warming theme. Among the special effects are that the temperature in the theater changes from 55 to 90 degrees during the film-*You freeze, you cook, you wish you'd planned ahead.*

The popcorn is oversalted. Before the tidal wave hits, I am panting with thirst. "Water," I whisper, climbing over her, into the aisle.

She pulls me back into my seat. "Don't go."

At key moments, she covers her eyes and waits until I squeeze her free hand to give her the all clear.

We are in the car on the way home. She is driving. The night is black. We move through the depths of darkness—the thin yellow line, the pathway home unfolds before us. There is the hum of the engine, the steadiness of her foot on the gas.

"We have to talk," I tell her.

"We talk constantly. We never stop talking."

"There's something I need to. . ." I say, not finishing the thought.

A deer crosses the road. My wife swerves. The car goes up a hill, trees fly by, the car goes down, we are rolling, we are hanging upsidedown, suspended, and then boom, we are back on our feet, the air bag smashes me in the face, punches me in the nose. The steering wheel explodes into her chest. We are down in a ditch with balloons pressed into our faces, suffocating.

"Are you hurt?" she asks.

"I'm fine," I say. "Are you all right?"

"Did we hit it?"

"No, I think it got away."

The doors unlock.

"I'm sorry," she says, "I'm so sorry. I didn't see it coming."

The air bags are slowly deflating—losing pressure.

"I want to live," I tell her. "I just don't know how."

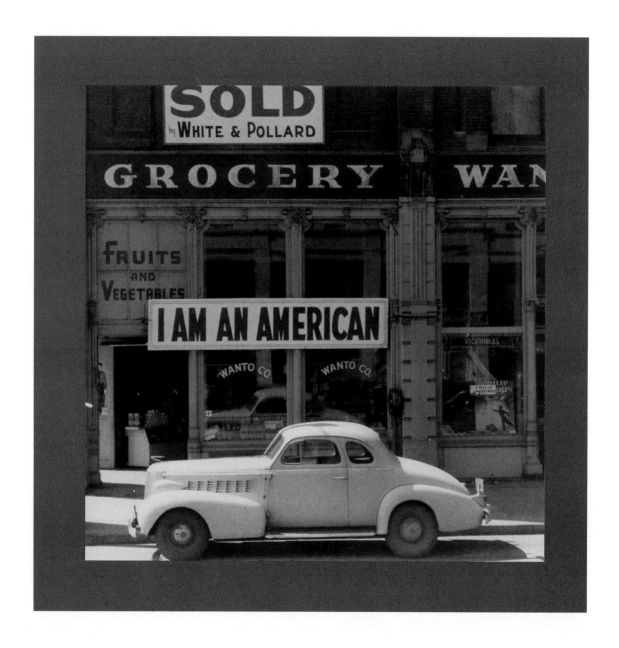

FOR THE JIM CROW MEXICAN RESTAURANT IN CAMBRIDGE, MASSACHUSETTS WHERE MY COUSIN ESTEBAN WAS FORBIDDEN TO WAIT TABLES BECAUSE HE WEARS DREADLOCKS

Martín Espada

I HAVE NOTICED THAT THE HOSTESS IN PEASANT DRESS,
the waitstaff and the boss
share the complexion of a flour tortilla.
I have spooked the servers at my table
by trilling the word burrito.
I am aware of your T-shirt solidarity
with the refugees of the Américas,
since they steam in your kitchen.
I know my cousin Esteban the sculptor
rolled tortillas in your kitchen
with the fingertips
of ancestral Puerto Rican cigar makers.
I understand he wanted to be a waiter,
but you proclaimed
his black dreadlocks unclean,
so he hissed in Spanish
and his apron collapsed on the floor.

May La Migra handcuff the waitstaff
as suspected illegal aliens from Canada;
may a hundred mice dive from the oven
like diminutive leaping dolphins
during your Board of Health inspection;
may the kitchen workers strike, sitting
with folded hands as enchiladas blacken
and twisters of smoke panic the customers;
may a Zapatista squadron
commandeer the refrigerator,
liberating a pillar of tortillas at gunpoint;
may you hallucinate dreadlocks
braided in thick vines round your ankles;
and may the Aztec gods pinned like butterflies
to the menu wait for you in the parking lot
at midnight, demanding
that you spell their names.

Left: The day after Pearl Harbor, orders were given for Japanese living in America to be evacuated. The owner of this shop in Oakland, California, who was a University of California graduate of Japanese descent, put this notice across his shop front.

T H E   B E A S T

William Golding
Excerpt from *Lord of the Flies*

THE AFTERNOON WORE ON, HAZY AND dreadful with damp heat; the sow staggered her way ahead of them, bleeding and mad, and the hunters followed, wedded to her in lust, excited by the long chase and the dropped blood. They could see her now, nearly got up with her, but she spurted with her last strength and held ahead of them again. They were just behind her when she staggered into an open space where bright flowers grew and butterflies danced round each other and the air was hot and still.

Here, struck down by the heat, the sow fell and the hunters hurled themselves at her. This dreadful eruption from an unknown world made her frantic; she squealed and bucked and the air was full of sweat and noise and blood and terror. Roger ran round the

Above: Chester Arnold, *A New Generation.*   **Right:** Phyllis Taplitz, *The Shark.* This is part of a series of works called *Contemporary Ruins* by Phyllis Taplitz. A statement of time, the cracked and decaying walls, chipped paint and rusting ironwork stand in patent contrast to recent graffiti offering the viewer a symbiotic relationship between the human imprint and nature.

heap, prodding with his spear whenever pigflesh appeared. Jack was on top of the sow, stabbing downward with his knife. Roger found a lodgment for his point and began to push till he was leaning with his whole weight. The spear moved forward inch by inch and the terrified squealing became a high-pitched scream. Then Jack found the throat and the hot blood spouted over his hands. The sow collapsed under them and they were heavy and fulfilled upon her. The butterflies still danced, preoccupied in the center of the clearing.

At last the immediacy of the kill subsided. The boys drew back, and Jack. . . paused and stood up, looking at the shadows under the trees. His voice was lower when he spoke again.

"But we'll leave part of the kill for . . ."

He knelt down again and was busy with his knife. The boys crowded round him. He spoke over his shoulder to Roger.

"Sharpen a stick at both ends."

Presently he stood up, holding the dripping sow's head in his hands.

"Where's that stick?"

"Here."

"Ram one end in the earth. Oh—it's rock. Jam it in that crack. There."

Jack held up the head and jammed the soft throat down on the pointed end of the stick which pierced through into the mouth. He stood back and the head hung there, a little blood dribbling down the stick.

Instinctively the boys drew back too; and the forest was very still. They listened, and the loudest noise was the buzzing of flies over the spilled guts.

Jack spoke in a whisper.

"Pick up the pig."

Maurice and Robert skewered the carcass, lifted the dead weight, and stood ready. In the silence, and standing over the dry blood, they looked suddenly furtive.

Jack spoke loudly.

"This head is for the beast. It's a gift."

The silence accepted the gift and awed them. The head remained there, dim-eyed, grinning faintly, blood blackening between the teeth. All at once they were running away, as fast as they could, through the forest toward the open beach.

S imon stayed where he was, a small brown image, concealed by the leaves. Even if he shut his eyes the sow's head still remained like an after-image. The half-shut eyes were dim with the infinite cynicism of adult life. They assured Simon that everything was a bad business.

"I know that."

Simon discovered that he had spoken aloud. He opened his eyes quickly and there was the head grinning amusedly in the strange daylight, ignoring the flies, the spilled guts, even ignoring the indignity of being spiked on a stick.

He looked away, licking his dry lips.

A gift for the beast. Might not the beast come for it? The head, he thought, appeared to agree with him. Run away, said the head silently, go back to the others. It was a joke really—why should you bother? You were just wrong, that's all. A little headache, something you ate, perhaps. Go back, child, said the head silently.

Simon looked up, feeling the weight of his wet hair, and gazed at the sky. Up there, for once, were clouds, great bulging towers that sprouted away over the island, grey and cream and copper-colored. The clouds were sitting on the land; they squeezed, produced moment by moment this close, tormenting heat. Even the butterflies deserted the open space where the obscene thing grinned and dripped. Simon lowered his head, carefully keeping his eyes shut, then sheltered them with his hand. There were no shadows under the trees but everywhere a pearly stillness, so that what was real seemed illusive and without definition. The pile of guts was a black blob of flies that buzzed like a saw. After a while these flies found Simon. Gorged, they alighted by his runnels of sweat and drank. They tickled under his nostrils and played leap-frog on his thighs. They were black and iridescent green and without number; and in front of Simon, the Lord of the Flies hung on his stick and grinned. At last Simon gave up and looked back; saw the white teeth and dim eyes, the blood—and his gaze was held by that ancient, inescapable recognition. In Simon's right temple, a pulse began to beat on the brain. . . .

"You are a silly little boy," said the Lord of the Flies, just an ignorant, silly little boy."

Simon moved his swollen tongue but said nothing.

"Don't you agree?' said the Lord of the Flies. "Aren't you just a silly little boy?"

Simon answered him in the same silent voice.

"Well then," said the Lord of the Flies, "you'd better run off and play with the others. They think you're batty. You don't want Ralph to think you're batty, do you? You like Ralph a lot, don't you? And Piggy, and Jack?"

Simon's head was tilted slightly up. His eyes could not break away and the Lord of the Flies hung in space before him.

"What are you doing out here all alone? Aren't you afraid of me?"

Simon shook.

"There isn't anyone to help you. Only me. And I'm the Beast."

Simon's mouth labored, brought forth audible words.

"Pig's head on a stick."

"Fancy thinking the Beast was something you could hunt and kill!" said the head. For a moment or two the forest and all the other dimly appreciated places echoed with the parody of laughter. "You knew, didn't you? I'm part of you? Close, close, close! I'm the reason why it's no go? Why things are what they are?"

The laughter shivered again.

"Come now," said the Lord of the Flies. "Get back to the others and we'll forget the whole thing."

Simon's head wobbled. His eyes were half closed as though he were imitating the obscene thing on the stick. He knew that one of his times was coming on. The Lord of the Flies was expanding like a balloon.

"This is ridiculous. You know perfectly well you'll only meet me down there—so don't try to escape!"

Simon's body was arched and stiff. The Lord of the Flies spoke in the voice of a schoolmaster.

"This has gone quite far enough. My poor, misguided child, do you think you know better than I do?"

There was a pause.

"I'm warning you. I'm going to get angry. D'you see? You're not wanted. Understand? We are going to have fun on this island. Understand? We are going to have fun on this island! So don't try it on, my poor misguided boy, or else—"

Simon found he was looking into a vast mouth. There was blackness within, a blackness that spread.

"—Or else," said the Lord of the Flies, "we shall do you. See? Jack and Roger and Maurice and Robert and Bill and Piggy and Ralph. Do you. See?"

Simon was inside the mouth. He fell down and lost consciousness.

Opposite: Chester Arnold, *Boar's Head.*

A C K N O W L E D G M E N T S

First and foremost, we would like to thank Jeremy Tarcher for his vision in creating this anthology series, and for his dedication and unwavering support in guiding the book towards completion. Our greatest appreciation is also extended to Robert Bly, Jean Houston, Robert A. Johnson, and Andrew Weil for their essential contributions to this series. To John Beebe, editor of the *San Francisco Institute Library Journal,* Alan B. Chinen, Connie Zweig, and the many members of the Jungian, transpersonal, and holistic medicine communities for their insights and suggestions concerning the selection of materials for these books—our deepest thanks. The talents of several people came together to make this unique collection of stories and art into the beautiful volume you hold in your hands. Mark Robert Waldman, whose skills as an author and editor shine in the choices he made for the book, carefully selected the texts. Julie Foakes, whose talents as an art researcher can never be praised enough, chose all the images. Marion Kocot brought order and harmony to the words with her talented editing skills. Sara Carder at Tarcher Putnam provided constant encouragement and handholding throughout the process. Joel Fontinos, the publisher at Tarcher Putnam, guided us with enthusiasm and praise. And Kristen Garneau brought text and images together in the elegant layout of the pages. To you all A HUGE THANK YOU!

—Philip and Manuela Dunn of The Book Laboratory Inc.

ABOUT THE EDITOR

Mark Robert Waldman is a therapist and the author and editor of numerous books, including *The Spirit of Writing, Love Games, Dreamscaping* and *The Art of Staying Together.* He was founding editor of *Transpersonal Review,* covering the fields of transpersonal and Jungian psychology, religious studies, and mind/body medicine.

ABOUT THE BOOK CREATORS

Philip Dunn and Manuela Dunn Mascetti have created many best-selling volumes, including *The Illustrated Rumi,* Huston Smith's *Illustrated World's Religions,* Stephen Hawking's *The Illustrated A Brief History of Time* and *The Universe in a Nutshell,* and Thomas Moore's *The Illustrated Care of the Soul.* They are the authors of *The Illustrated Rumi, The Buddha Box,* and many other books.

ABOUT THE INTRODUCTORY AUTHOR

Robert Bly is an American Poet Laureate who has authored, edited and translated numerous books of poetry and prose, including *A Little Book on the Human Shadow, Iron John: A Book About Men, The Rag and Bone Shop, Loving a Woman in Two Worlds* and *The Sibling Society.*

T E X T   A C K N O W L E D G M E N T S

Every effort has been made to trace all copyright holders of the material included in this volume, whether companies or individuals. Any omission is unintentional and we will be pleased to correct any errors in future editions of this book.

Children of Strikers, ©1980 by Fred Chappell has been reprinted by kind permission of the author.

The Dead Boy at the Window, © 1998 by Bruce Holland Rogers, first appeared in The North American Review, and reprinted here by kind permission of the author.

Direct Male, © 2000 by Risa Mickenberg, reproduced by kind permission of the author.

Diving Into the Wreck, from *Diving Into the Wreck: Poems 1971-1972* by Adrienne Rich, ©1973 by W. W. Norton & Company, Inc. Reprinted by kind permission of the author and W. W. Norton & Company, Inc.

The Hand of God, © 1975 by Howard Fast, reprinted by kind permission of Sterling Lord Literistic, Inc.

For the Jim Crow Mexican Restaurant in Cambridge, Massachusetts Where My Cousin Esteban Was Forbidden to Wait Tables Because He Wears Dreadlock, © 2000 by Martín Espada. Reprinted from *A Mayan Astronomer in Hell's Kitchen,* and published by W.W. Norton, 2000, reprinted by kind permission of the author.

Four Dark Tales by Joyce Carol Oates, © 2002 by Ontario Review Press Inc. Reprinted by kind permission of John Hawkins & Associates, Inc.

A R T A C K N O W L E D G M E N T S

Page 11   Chester Arnold, *Genealogy,* oil on canvas, 66" x 80", photo credit: Jacques G. Cressaty

Page 16   Leonard Baskin, *The Old Artist,* Reynolda House, Museum of American Art, Winston-Salem, North Carolina

Page 18   Burning Man 2001, photography by Tony Pletts

Page 19   © Jane Zich, *Chained Melody,* mixed media on paper, 9" x 12"

Page 23   Alfonso Ossorio, *Scavenger's Heart,* 1944, watercolor on paper, Sheet: 14" x 20", Whitney Museum of American Art, New York; gift of the artist, 69.152. © Ossorio Foundation, Southampton, NY, courtesy of Michael Rosenfeld Gallery, New York, NY

Page 24   © Jane Zich, *Into Dreams,* pen and ink on paper, 5" x 7"

Page 26   Cathryn Chase, *Halloween Chill*

Page 29   Chester Arnold, *TWA Corbies,* oil on linen, 72" x 60", photo credit: Jacques G. Cressaty

Page 31   Chester Arnold, *After the Fall,* oil on linen, 60" x 72", photo credit: Jacques G. Cressaty

Page 34   Andrew Lane

Page 40   Cathryn Chase, *Lookout*

Page 45   Grant Wood, American, 1891-1942, *American Gothic,* 1930, oil on beaverboard, 74.3 x 62.4 cm, Friends of American Art Collection, All rights reserved by The Art Institute of Chicago and VAGA, New York, NY, 1930.934, photo reproduction © The Art Institute of Chicago. All Rights Reserved

Page 46   Andrew Lane

Page 50   Aaron Bohrod, *Hilltop Farm,* Lodi, Wisconsin, Reynolda House, Museum of American Art, Winston-Salem, North Carolina

Page 58   Cathryn Chase, *Gate*

Page 62   Georgia O'Keeffe, American, 1887-1986. *Cow's Skull with Calico Roses,* 1932, oil on canvas, 92.2 x 61.3 cm, Gift of Georgia O'Keeffe, 1947.712, photo reproduction © The Art Institute of Chicago. All Rights Reserved

Page 64 &
details page 66   Getty Images/Hulton Archive

Page 68   Getty Images/Hulton Archive

Page 70   Horace Pippin, *The Whipping;* Reynolda House, Museum of American Art, Winston-Salem, North Carolina

Page 75   Getty Images/Hulton Archive

Page 76   Getty Images/Hulton Archive

Page 79   © Jane Zich, *The Judges,* pen and ink on paper, 5" x 7"

Page 80   Phyllis Taplitz, *Triangle of Light,* encaustic on canvas, 30" x 42"

Page 81   Getty Images/Hulton Archive

Page 85   John Marin, *Downtown, NY;* Reynolda House, Museum of American Art, Winston-Salem, North Carolina

Page 86   Getty Images/Hulton Archive

Page 87   Getty Images/Hulton Archive

Page 90   Paul LaMantia, American, b. 1938, *Day Thru Evening Dream,* 1984, oil on canvas, 1984.178, photo reproduction © The Art Institute of Chicago. All Rights Reserved

Page 125   Getty Images/Hulton Archive

Page 128   Mark Tobey, American, 1890-1976, *Above the Earth,* 1953, gouache, 100.3 x 75.6 cm, gift
                of Mrs. Sigmund Kunstadter, 1953.340, photo reproduction © The Art Institute of Chicago.
                All Rights Reserved

Page 130   Georgia O'Keeffe, *Dark Mesa with Pink Sky,* 1930, oil on canvas, 1965.80; Amon Carter
                Museum, Fort Worth, Texas

Page 131   John Henshaw, *Driver-NYC*

Page 137   John Rogers Cox, American, 1915-1990, *Gray & Gold,* 1942. Oil on canvas, 91.5 x 151.8
                cm. © The Cleveland Museum of Art, 2002. Mr. and Mrs. William H. Marlatt Fund, 1943.60

Page 140   Getty Images/Hulton Archive

Page 142   Chester Arnold, *A New Generation,* oil on canvas, 70" x 96", photo credit: Jacques G.
                Cressaty

Page 143   Phyllis Taplitz, *The Shark,* oil pastel on paper, 30" x 40"

Page 147   Chester Arnold, *Boar's Head,* oil on board, 14" x 16"

Cover art: Richard Hess, *Reflections?,* Painting by HessDesignWorks.com.